D1736764

Fatty Liver Detox Cookbook

Elevate Your Health Journey with Flavourful, Nutritious Recipes and Essential Dietary Strategies for Transformative Wellbeing and Energy.

By Dane Delarosa

Table Of Contents

DOWNLOAD YOUR BONUS

RENAL DIET RECIPES

Dear Reader,

Thank you so much for purchasing my book and downloading the bonus! I hope you find it insightful and valuable. If you enjoyed the book, we would greatly appreciate it if you could take a moment to leave a review on Amazon.
Your feedback is incredibly important to me and helps other readers discover our work.

With gratitude,

Dane Delarosa

Chapter 1: Understanding Fatty Liver Disease

The Liver: Functions and Importance

In the shelter of our ribcage lies an unsung hero, the liver, a tireless guardian of our internal equilibrium. This vital organ, often overshadowed by its more vocal counterparts, performs an astonishing array of tasks essential to our survival and well-being. It's not merely an organ; it's a hub of activity, a cornerstone of health, and a testament to the body's remarkable capacity for balance and renewal.

Consider its role as the body's chemical processing plant. Here, it tirelessly toils, converting nutrients from the foods we savor into life-sustaining substances, detoxifying harmful compounds, and managing an intricate dance of hormones and enzymes. It's a master of metabolism, overseeing the conversion of food into fuel and tirelessly working to maintain a steady supply of energy to every cell in our body.

Its detoxifying feats are nothing short of heroic. Every toxin, every medication, and every drop of alcohol we consume passes under its vigilant scrutiny. With precision and efficiency, it breaks down these substances, rendering them harmless or preparing them for safe elimination. This process is continuous, a testament to its unwavering commitment to our health.

But its duties extend far beyond detoxification and metabolism. It's a vital contributor to blood health, producing essential proteins and factors that help our blood clot, protecting us from excessive bleeding and facilitating healing. It stores vitamins and minerals, releasing them into the bloodstream as needed, ensuring that our cells are nourished and our bodies remain robust.

Even its physical resilience is remarkable. It possesses the extraordinary ability to regenerate itself, to repair and rebuild after injury. This capacity is a beacon of hope in the face of liver disease, reminding us of the body's profound potential for healing and recovery.

Yet, despite its vital roles, it's often only when things go awry that we recognize its importance. When its function is impaired, the effects can be far-reaching and profound, affecting every aspect of our health and well-being. This is why understanding and appreciating its role is not just an academic pursuit; it's a crucial aspect of living a healthy, balanced life.

As we embark on this journey through the complexities of fatty liver disease and the myriad ways we can support this vital organ, let's do so with a newfound respect and appreciation for all it does. Let's remember that each choice we make, from the foods we eat to the lifestyle we lead, is an opportunity to support its function and honor its essential role in our lives.

What is Fatty Liver Disease? Types and Causes

In the realm of human health, few conditions are as insidiously silent yet progressively perilous as fatty liver disease, a stealthy usurper of liver wellness. This ailment, characterized by an excessive accumulation of fat within the liver cells, is not a mere inconvenience; it's a growing concern in the medical community, reflecting broader issues of lifestyle, diet, and health management prevalent in contemporary society.

At its core, fatty liver disease, or hepatic steatosis, signifies a betrayal of the organ's faithful service. The liver, typically a paragon of detoxification and metabolic management, finds itself infiltrated by an overabundance of fat. This condition is not about the organ's own fat creation but rather a consequence of various external factors and internal dysfunctions that lead to fat accumulation.

The spectrum of fatty liver disease is broad, encompassing two primary types: non-alcoholic fatty liver disease (NAFLD) and its more intoxicating counterpart, alcoholic liver disease (ALD). NAFLD, the more prevalent form, occurs in individuals who consume little to no alcohol. It's a reflection of modern maladies - a sedentary lifestyle, overnutrition, and metabolic disorders. Within NAFLD itself, there are further classifications, ranging from benign fat accumulation to non-alcoholic steatohepatitis (NASH), a more aggressive state that may progress to cirrhosis or liver cancer if left unchecked.

On the other side, ALD is a testament to the destructive potential of chronic alcohol abuse. Here, the liver becomes a victim of excessive alcoholic consumption, struggling under the toxic effects of alcohol metabolism. It's a stark reminder of the delicate balance of health and the profound impact of our choices.

The causative factors behind fatty liver are as diverse as they are interconnected. For many, it's the consequence of obesity and insulin resistance, part of the metabolic syndrome constellation that includes hypertension and hyperlipidemia. The liver becomes a depot for the excess triglycerides circulating in the body, a storage unit overwhelmed by the sheer volume of fat.

Yet, the story of fatty liver is not one of single culprits but rather a complex interplay of genetic predisposition, lifestyle choices, and environmental influences. Some individuals might inherit a tendency towards inefficient fat metabolism, making their livers more vulnerable to fat accumulation. Others might find their liver health compromised by rapid weight loss, certain medications, or underlying health conditions like type 2 diabetes.

The journey from a healthy liver to one burdened by fat is typically a silent one. In the early stages, fatty liver is often a quiet condition, lurking undetected and asymptomatic. It's only as the condition progresses, as the liver swells and its function falters, that symptoms might emerge. Even then, they are often vague and easily dismissed—fatigue, a dull ache in the upper right abdomen, unexplained weight loss or weakness.

Symptoms and Diagnosis of Fatty Liver

Initially, fatty liver tends to be a silent affair, with many individuals experiencing no discernible symptoms. It's a covert operator, causing few ripples on the surface while potentially setting the stage for more significant health issues. However, as the condition progresses, it may begin to whisper its presence through a constellation of subtle signs. Individuals might experience a sense of fatigue that's not just the result of a long day but a persistent weariness that clings and slows. Some might notice a dull, aching sensation in the upper right abdomen, where the liver resides - a gentle yet persistent reminder that all is not well within.

For others, discomfort might manifest in unexplained weight loss or a feeling of fullness, a physical declaration of the liver's struggle. As the organ becomes increasingly infiltrated with fat, it may enlarge, leading to a condition known as hepatomegaly, which can be detected by a healthcare professional during a physical examination. However, these signs are often nebulous and can be easily attributed to a myriad of less serious conditions, leading many to overlook their liver health until more severe complications arise.

The journey to a definitive diagnosis typically begins with suspicion, often arising during routine examinations or while investigating other health concerns. A physician, noting the subtle hints or risk factors, might delve deeper, employing a range of diagnostic tools to peek beneath the surface. Blood tests may reveal elevated liver enzymes, indicators of inflammation and damage to liver cells. Yet, these tests are not exclusive to fatty liver and can only suggest the possibility of liver dysfunction.

Imaging studies offer a more direct gaze into the liver's condition. Ultrasound, a non-invasive and widely accessible technique, can detect increased fat in the liver, presenting a safe and effective first step in diagnosis. For a more detailed view, computed tomography (CT) or magnetic resonance imaging (MRI) might be employed, offering a clearer picture of the liver's structure and the extent of fat infiltration.

In cases where uncertainty lingers or when the assessment of liver damage is crucial, a liver biopsy might be performed. This procedure, though more invasive, provides a definitive diagnosis and a clear view of the liver's condition, revealing not just the presence of fat but also the extent of inflammation, fibrosis, or scarring.

The diagnosis of fatty liver is thus a journey of detection and understanding, a critical phase in the narrative of health where the silent progression of the disease meets the clarity of medical insight. It's a point of convergence between the individual's experience and the broader knowledge of medicine, where subtle symptoms lead to definitive tests, and the hidden story of the liver begins to unfold.

The Role of Diet in Managing Fatty Liver

The culinary journey towards a healthier liver is not about stringent deprivation but rather about informed, thoughtful choices that nurture and support liver function. It is a shift towards a diet rich in whole, unprocessed foods that minimize the liver's workload and maximize its ability to heal and regenerate.

At the heart of this dietary shift is the reduction of excess dietary fats, particularly saturated fats and trans fats, which can exacerbate liver fat accumulation. Instead, the focus turns to incorporating healthy fats, such as those found in avocados, nuts, and olive oil, which support overall health without overburdening the liver. These fats are not just an energy source; they are building blocks for recovery and health, fostering a balanced and nurturing dietary environment.

Simultaneously, a significant reduction in refined sugars and simple carbohydrates is paramount. These foods cause spikes in blood sugar and insulin levels, contributing to fat accumulation and insulin resistance, a common accomplice in the progression of fatty liver disease. In their place, a bounty of fiber-rich fruits, vegetables, and whole grains take center stage, providing the liver with the nutrients it needs to function optimally and the body with a sustained, gentle source of energy.

Protein plays a pivotal role as well, with a focus on lean sources like poultry, fish, and plant-based proteins. These nutrients support the liver's repair and maintenance processes without the excessive fat and calories that can exacerbate liver issues. Moreover, proteins are essential in supporting the liver's detoxification pathways, ensuring that it can effectively neutralize and eliminate toxins from the body.

In addition to what is eaten, how one eats also holds significance. Smaller, more frequent meals can help manage blood sugar levels and reduce the liver's workload, allowing it to process nutrients more effectively and maintain stable energy levels. Hydration, too, is key, as water helps to flush toxins from the body and supports overall liver function.

Beyond specific foods, the dietary approach to managing fatty liver involves an overall pattern of eating that emphasizes balance, variety, and moderation. It's a holistic shift that integrates the principles of nutritious eating with the unique needs of those managing fatty liver disease. This approach is not about short-term diets or quick fixes; it's about sustainable, enjoyable changes that promote liver health and overall well-being.

Chapter 2: Fundamentals of the Liver Detox Diet

Principles of a Liver-Friendly Diet

Embarking on the journey to support and rejuvenate the liver through dietary means requires a compass of principles that guide each meal choice, snack selection, and even the sip of a beverage. A liver-friendly diet isn't a fleeting fad or a draconian regime; it's a sustainable, enjoyable, and healthful way of eating that honors the liver's critical functions and its pivotal role in overall health.

Central to this dietary approach is the principle of nourishment without overburdening. The liver, your body's vigilant detoxifier and metabolic powerhouse, thrives on a balanced mix of nutrients while being vulnerable to excess and toxins. Thus, the diet that favors liver health is rich in whole, unprocessed foods that deliver maximum nutritional value with minimal toxic impact. These foods are the liver's allies, supporting its functions and easing its load.

A liver-friendly diet emphasizes the importance of quality and variety. It favors lean proteins, whole grains, and an abundance of fresh fruits and vegetables. Lean proteins from poultry, fish, and plant sources provide essential amino acids without excess fat. Whole grains offer complex carbohydrates and fiber, which aid in digestion and steady blood sugar management. Fruits and vegetables are treasure troves of vitamins, minerals, antioxidants, and fiber, which not only support liver function but also enhance the body's overall health.

Fats are not shunned but chosen wisely. Healthy fats, such as those found in avocados, nuts, seeds, and olive oil, provide energy and support cell growth without taxing the liver. These fats are integral to a balanced diet, contributing to satiety, flavor, and nutrient absorption.

Hydration is another cornerstone of a liver-friendly diet. Water helps flush toxins from the body and maintains proper digestion and nutrient transport. It is the essence of life and the medium through which the liver performs its myriad of biochemical reactions.

Mindful eating is also integral to this approach. It's about listening to the body's hunger and fullness cues, eating slowly, and savoring each bite. This mindfulness enhances digestion and absorption of nutrients, ensuring that the liver receives a steady, manageable supply of what it needs to function optimally.

Portion control is the subtle art of respecting the body's needs without imposing excess. It's about understanding the fine balance between nourishment and overindulgence, ensuring that each meal contributes to health without overwhelming the liver with excessive calories or harmful substances.

Lastly, a liver-friendly diet is adaptable and personal. It recognizes individual needs, preferences, and lifestyles, offering flexibility within the framework of liver health. It's a diet that evolves with you, accommodating changes in health status, lifestyle, and even taste preferences.

As you embark on this path, remember that a liver-friendly diet is more than a collection of food choices; it's a commitment to nurturing and respecting your body's incredible resilience and complexity.

Nutrients Essential for Liver Health

In the pursuit of liver wellness, understanding the essential nutrients that support the liver's multifaceted roles is like mapping the treasures necessary for its optimum functioning. These nutrients are the building blocks and facilitators of the liver's intricate processes, helping it to detoxify, metabolize, and repair itself.

Firstly, antioxidants stand as vigilant protectors against oxidative stress, a relentless assailant of liver cells. Vitamins such as vitamin E and vitamin C are potent antioxidants. Vitamin E, found in nuts, seeds, and green leafy vegetables, protects the liver's cell membranes from damage. Similarly, vitamin C, abundant in fruits like oranges, strawberries, and kiwi, contributes to the liver's defense against oxidative stress and helps in regenerating other antioxidants within the body.

Transitioning from antioxidants, let's consider the role of B-vitamins, particularly B12, B6, and folate. These vitamins are paramount in the liver's metabolic processes, aiding in detoxification and energy production. B-vitamins are involved in converting homocysteine into methionine, an amino acid essential for liver repair and function. Good sources of B-vitamins include whole grains, legumes, and animal products like dairy and meat.

Next, amino acids, the building blocks of proteins, are vital for liver function. They assist in detoxification pathways and tissue repair. Amino acids like methionine, cysteine, and taurine are particularly noteworthy for their roles in synthesizing glutathione, a powerful antioxidant crucial for detoxification within the liver. To ensure an adequate supply of these amino acids, include a variety of protein sources in your diet, such as lean meats, fish, eggs, and plant-based proteins like lentils and quinoa.

Moreover, the importance of trace elements like zinc and selenium in liver health cannot be overstated. Zinc helps in the metabolism of alcohol and other substances processed by the liver. It's also a component of many enzymes necessary for liver function. Selenium, on the other hand, works closely with antioxidants to protect the liver cells from damage. These trace elements are found in nuts, seeds, seafood, and whole grains.

Furthermore, omega-3 fatty acids, typically found in fatty fish, flaxseeds, and walnuts, are known for their anti-inflammatory properties. They help in reducing liver fat and inflammation, a common feature in fatty liver disease. Incorporating omega-3 rich foods into your diet can support the liver's health and its ability to respond to and recover from damage.

Lastly, fiber plays a subtle yet significant role in liver health. By aiding digestion and ensuring a steady absorption of nutrients, fiber helps in maintaining a healthy gut flora. A well-functioning digestive system reduces the liver's workload and supports its detoxification efforts. Foods high in fiber such as fruits, vegetables, whole grains, and legumes should be a regular feature in a liver-friendly diet.

Foods to Include and Avoid for Liver Detox

Firstly, let's illuminate the foods that are beneficial allies in liver detoxification. These are the nutritional heroes, packed with antioxidants, vitamins, minerals, and fibers, ready to support the liver's intricate detox pathways. Leafy greens such as spinach, kale, and chard are loaded with chlorophyll, which assists in purging toxins from the bloodstream and boosting liver function. Similarly, cruciferous vegetables like broccoli, Brussels sprouts, and cauliflower contain glucosinolates, enhancing the liver's enzyme production and aiding in toxin removal.

Moreover, fruits are not to be overlooked; berries, oranges, and grapes come laden with antioxidants and vitamins. They offer a sweet arsenal against the oxidative stress that the liver encounters daily. Citrus fruits, in particular, are rich in vitamin C and compounds that bolster liver health, encouraging the cleansing process. Additionally, the inclusion of nuts, rich in omega-3 fatty acids and amino acids, supports liver cleansing while providing a hearty dose of essential nutrients.

Transitioning smoothly, it's equally crucial to recognize the foods that pose challenges to liver health. Foremost among these are processed and fried foods, notorious for their high levels of unhealthy fats and additives. These culprits are laden with trans fats and refined sugars that burden the liver with extra work in detoxification and fat metabolism. Regular consumption can lead to an accumulation of unhealthy fat within the liver, exacerbating the risk of fatty liver disease.

Moreover, excessive alcohol consumption is a well-known antagonist to liver health. It overwhelms the liver's ability to process and detoxify, leading to fat accumulation, inflammation, and even scarring. Minimizing or eliminating alcohol intake is a significant step towards liver detox and overall health.

Additionally, red meat and high-fat dairy products, while occasionally acceptable in moderation, are typically high in saturated fats. When consumed in excess, they contribute to increased cholesterol levels and liver burden. Opting for lean proteins and low-fat dairy options provides the body with necessary nutrients without the extra fat that hampers liver function.

Now, as we further refine our understanding, it's important to note that balance and moderation are key. While certain foods are undoubtedly beneficial for liver health, overconsumption of even the healthiest foods can lead to imbalance and stress on the liver. Similarly, an occasional indulgence in less healthy foods isn't likely to cause harm if the overall dietary pattern is focused on liver health. The goal is to consistently make choices that support detoxification and liver function, creating a diet that is varied, enjoyable, and sustainable.

Lifestyle Changes to Support Liver Health

As we continue our exploration of liver health, it becomes clear that beyond diet, a constellation of lifestyle choices casts significant influence over the well-being of this vital organ. These choices, ranging from physical activity to stress management, are not isolated actions but threads in the larger tapestry of liver health.

First and foremost, engaging in regular physical activity stands out as a critical pillar supporting the liver. Exercise not only aids in weight management—thus reducing the risk of fatty liver disease—but also improves insulin sensitivity and stimulates metabolism. It's like a gentle nudge, encouraging the liver to maintain its detoxifying and metabolic efficiency. Whether it's brisk walking, cycling, swimming, or any other form of activity that raises the heart rate, the key is consistency and enjoyment, making it a sustainable part of one's routine.

Transitioning from physical activity, managing stress effectively is another essential aspect of a liver-friendly lifestyle. Chronic stress can lead to behaviors that burden the liver, such as overeating or alcohol consumption, and directly impact its function through the prolonged release of stress hormones. Techniques such as mindfulness meditation, deep breathing exercises, or engaging in hobbies can significantly mitigate stress and create a more liver-friendly internal environment.

Moreover, adequate sleep is a crucial yet often overlooked component of liver health. During sleep, the body, including the liver, goes into repair and rejuvenation mode. Disruptions in sleep patterns or inadequate rest can impede these vital processes, leading to increased stress and inefficiency in the liver's functions.

Cultivating good sleep hygiene—such as maintaining a regular sleep schedule, creating a restful environment, and limiting screen time before bed—can enhance liver health along with overall well-being.

Additionally, avoiding toxins is fundamental to protecting the liver. This includes minimizing or eliminating alcohol consumption, as well as being mindful of the intake of over-the-counter medications and other substances that can be taxing on the liver. It's about making conscious choices, recognizing the potential impact of various substances, and seeking alternatives or moderation wherever possible.

In conclusion, supporting liver health is an integrated endeavor, one that extends beyond diet into the broader realms of physical activity, stress management, sleep, and avoidance of toxins. Each of these lifestyle factors offers an avenue to bolster the liver's functions, creating a more resilient and healthy organ. As we incorporate these changes into our lives, they collectively contribute to a stronger, more vibrant liver, capable of meeting the demands placed upon it.

Chapter 3: Breakfast Recipes for Liver Health

Energizing Smoothies and Juices for Liver Health

Green Detox Elixir

- **P.T.:** 10 mins
- **Ingr.:** 1 cup fresh spinach, 1 small cucumber, 1 green apple, 1/2 lemon (juiced), 1 tablespoon chia seeds, 1 cup coconut water.
- **Procedure:** Blend all ingredients until smooth. Enjoy immediately for maximum freshness and nutrient retention.
- **N.V.:** Rich in antioxidants, vitamins A and C, and fiber.
- **Suggestions:** Drink in the morning to kickstart liver detoxification processes and energize your day.

Beetroot Bliss Juice

- **P.T.:** 8 mins
- **Ingr.:** 1 medium beetroot, 2 carrots, 1/2 inch ginger root, 1 apple, 1/2 lemon (juiced).
- **Procedure:** Juice all ingredients, stirring in the lemon juice last. Serve chilled.
- **N.V.:** High in betalains, vitamin C, and potassium.
- **Suggestions:** Consume 2-3 times a week for optimal liver function and blood purification.

Turmeric Sunrise Smoothie

- **P.T.:** 7 mins
- **Ingr.:** 1 cup mango chunks, 1/2 banana, 1/2 teaspoon turmeric powder, 1 tablespoon flaxseeds, 1 cup almond milk.

- **Procedure:** Blend all ingredients until creamy. Adjust consistency with more almond milk if needed.
- **N.V.:** Loaded with curcumin, omega-3s, and vitamin E.
- **Suggestions:** Ideal for reducing inflammation and supporting liver detox.

Berry Liver Cleanse Shake

- **P.T.:** 9 mins
- **Ingr.:** 1 cup mixed berries (strawberries, blueberries, raspberries), 1 cup Greek yogurt, 1 tablespoon honey, 1/2 cup ice, 1 tablespoon almond butter.
- **Procedure:** Blend all ingredients until smooth. Taste and add honey for sweetness if desired.

- **N.V.:** Rich in antioxidants, probiotics, and healthy fats.
- **Suggestions:** A delicious and nutritious way to support liver health and digestion.

Avocado & Mint Refreshment

- **P.T.:** 6 mins
- **Ingr.:** 1 ripe avocado, 10 fresh mint leaves, 1 lime (juiced), 1 tablespoon honey, 1 cup water or almond milk.
- **Procedure:** Blend all ingredients until smooth, adding more water or almond milk to reach desired consistency.
- **N.V.:** High in healthy fats, fiber, and vitamin C.
- **Suggestions:** Drink this creamy smoothie as a filling breakfast or afternoon snack to aid in liver detoxification and boost energy levels.

Protein-Packed Breakfasts for Liver Health

Mediterranean Morning Scramble

- **P.T.:** 12 mins
- **Ingr.:** 2 large eggs, 1/4 cup diced tomatoes, 1/4 cup chopped spinach, 2 tbsp crumbled feta cheese, 1 tbsp olive oil, salt, and pepper to taste.
- **Procedure:** Heat olive oil in a pan. Add tomatoes and spinach, sautéing until wilted. Whisk eggs and pour over vegetables, cooking until set. Sprinkle feta cheese on top and season with salt and pepper.
- **N.V.:** High in protein, vitamins A and C, and healthy fats.
- **Suggestions:** Serve with a slice of whole-grain toast for a balanced meal.

Soy-Ginger Tofu Bowl

- **P.T.:** 15 mins
- **Ingr.:** 1/2 block firm tofu, 1 tbsp soy sauce, 1 tsp ginger, grated, 1 cup mixed bell peppers, sliced, 1 tbsp sesame oil, 1 green onion, chopped.
- **Procedure:** Drain and press tofu to remove excess water. Cut into cubes. Heat sesame oil in a pan, add tofu and vegetables, sautéing until golden. Add soy sauce and ginger, stirring well. Garnish with green onions.
- **N.V.:** Rich in plant-based protein, antioxidants, and iron.
- **Suggestions:** Enjoy this savory dish for a filling, liver-friendly start to your day.

Quinoa & Black Bean Breakfast Wrap

- **P.T.:** 20 mins
- **Ingr.:** 1/2 cup cooked quinoa, 1/4 cup black beans, 1 small avocado, sliced, 2 whole wheat tortillas, 1/4 cup salsa, salt, and pepper to taste.
- **Procedure:** Warm the tortillas. Lay out the tortillas and spread cooked quinoa, black beans, and avocado slices in the center. Add salsa, then fold into wraps. Heat on a skillet until slightly crispy.
- **N.V.:** High in fiber, protein, and essential fatty acids.
- **Suggestions:** A hearty, flavorful wrap perfect for on-the-go mornings.

Almond Butter & Banana Chia Pudding

- **P.T.:** Overnight + 10 mins
- **Ingr.:** 1/4 cup chia seeds, 1 cup unsweetened almond milk, 1 banana, sliced, 2 tbsp almond butter, 1 tsp honey (optional).
- **Procedure:** Mix chia seeds with almond milk, let sit overnight. Stir in almond butter and honey the next morning, top with banana slices.
- **N.V.:** Packed with omega-3s, potassium, and fiber.
- **Suggestions:** Prepare in individual jars for an easy, transportable breakfast.

Smoked Salmon and Avocado Omelette

- **P.T.:** 10 mins
- **Ingr.:** 2 large eggs, 2 slices smoked salmon, 1/2 ripe avocado, sliced, 1 tbsp chopped dill, salt, and pepper to taste.
- **Procedure:** Beat eggs and pour into a heated, oiled skillet. Cook until nearly set, then lay salmon and avocado slices on one half. Fold over, cooking until eggs are fully set. Season and garnish with dill.
- **N.V.:** High in omega-3 fatty acids, protein, and healthy fats.
- **Suggestions:** Serve immediately for a luxurious, nutritious start to your day.

Light and Nutritious Cereals for Liver Health

Ancient Grains Liver Boost Bowl

- **P.T.:** 15 mins
- **Ingr.:** 1/2 cup cooked amaranth, 1/4 cup cooked quinoa, 1 tbsp pumpkin seeds, 1/4 cup blueberries, 1 tbsp ground flaxseed, almond milk.
- **Procedure:** Combine amaranth and quinoa in a bowl. Top with pumpkin seeds, blueberries, and ground flaxseed. Pour almond milk as desired.
- **N.V.:** High in omega-3 fatty acids, antioxidants, and complete protein.
- **Suggestions:** Ideal for a filling, fiber-rich start to the day, supporting liver function and digestion.

Spiced Oat and Chia Porridge

- **P.T.:** 10 mins
- **Ingr.:** 1/2 cup rolled oats, 1 tbsp chia seeds, 1/2 tsp cinnamon, a pinch of nutmeg, 1 cup almond milk, 1 tbsp honey.
- **Procedure:** In a pot, combine oats, chia seeds, cinnamon, nutmeg, and almond milk. Cook over medium heat until thick. Drizzle with honey before serving.
- **N.V.:** Rich in fiber, omega-3 fatty acids, and anti-inflammatory properties.
- **Suggestions:** A warm, comforting breakfast that supports liver health and stabilizes blood sugar.

Tropical Buckwheat Bliss

- **P.T.:** 20 mins
- **Ingr.:** 1/2 cup buckwheat groats, 1 cup coconut milk, 1/2 mango, diced, 1/4 cup sliced strawberries, 1 tbsp coconut flakes.
- **Procedure:** Cook buckwheat in coconut milk until tender. Allow to cool, then top with mango, strawberries, and coconut flakes.

- **N.V.:** Provides a good source of plant protein, fiber, and vitamin C.
- **Suggestions:** An exotic, nutritious cereal that's perfect for liver detoxification.

Berry Walnut Muesli Mix

- **P.T.:** Overnight + 5 mins
- **Ingr.:** 1/2 cup rolled oats, 1/4 cup chopped walnuts, 1/4 cup mixed berries, 1 tbsp chia seeds, 1 cup Greek yogurt.

- **Procedure:** Mix oats, walnuts, berries, and chia seeds with Greek yogurt. Refrigerate overnight. Stir well before serving.
- **N.V.:** High in antioxidants, probiotics, and omega-3 fatty acids.
- **Suggestions:** A cold, creamy cereal that supports liver health and gut microbiome.

Golden Millet Power Porridge

- **P.T.:** 25 mins
- **Ingr.:** 1/2 cup millet, 1/2 tsp turmeric, 1/4 tsp ginger powder, 1 cup almond milk, 1 tbsp almond slivers, 1/2 banana, sliced.
- **Procedure:** Cook millet with turmeric, ginger, and almond milk until soft. Serve topped with almond slivers and banana slices.
- **N.V.:** Excellent source of B vitamins, fiber, and anti-inflammatory properties.
- **Suggestions:** A warming, nutrient-dense breakfast ideal for liver health and detoxification.

Liver Detoxifying Herbal Teas for Liver Health

Dandelion Root Detox Tea

- **P.T.:** 10 mins
- **Ingr.:** 1 tbsp dried dandelion root, 1 cup boiling water, 1 tsp honey (optional).
- **Procedure:** Steep dandelion root in boiling water for 10 minutes. Strain and add honey for sweetness if desired.
- **N.V.:** Rich in antioxidants and naturally supports liver detoxification.
- **Suggestions:** Drink this earthy tea in the morning to stimulate liver function.

Milk Thistle Sipper

- **P.T.:** 8 mins
- **Ingr.:** 1 tsp milk thistle seeds, 1 cup hot water, a slice of lemon.
- **Procedure:** Crush milk thistle seeds slightly and steep in hot water for 8 minutes. Add a slice of lemon before serving.
- **N.V.:** Known for liver-protecting silymarin content.
- **Suggestions:** Ideal for daily consumption to aid in liver health maintenance.

Ginger-Licorice Liver Elixir

- **P.T.:** 12 mins
- **Ingr.:** 1/2 inch ginger root, 1 tsp licorice root, 1 cup water, 1 tsp lemon juice.
- **Procedure:** Boil ginger and licorice in water for 10 minutes. Strain, add lemon juice, and serve warm.
- **N.V.:** Anti-inflammatory and soothing for the digestive system.
- **Suggestions:** Perfect as a post-meal beverage to enhance digestion and liver function.

Peppermint Liver Cleanse Tea

- **P.T.:** 5 mins
- **Ingr.:** 1 tbsp fresh peppermint leaves, 1 cup boiling water, 1 tsp honey (optional).
- **Procedure:** Steep peppermint leaves in boiling water for 5 minutes. Strain and sweeten with honey if desired.
- **N.V.:** Aids in bile production and digestion.
- **Suggestions:** Enjoy this refreshing tea in the afternoon for a gentle liver cleanse.

Turmeric and Cinnamon Blend

- **P.T.:** 10 mins
- **Ingr.:** 1/2 tsp turmeric powder, 1/4 tsp cinnamon, 1 cup water, 1 tsp honey.
- **Procedure:** Simmer turmeric and cinnamon in water for 8 minutes. Strain and add honey to taste.
- **N.V.:** Contains curcumin and antioxidants beneficial for liver health.
- **Suggestions:** Consume this warming tea in the evening to support liver detox and relaxation.

Chapter 4: Healthy and Hearty Lunches

Liver-Cleansing Salad Recipes for Healthy Lunches

Arugula and Beetroot Detox Salad

- **P.T.:** 15 mins
- **Ingr.:** 2 cups arugula, 1 medium beetroot (roasted and sliced), 1/4 cup walnuts, 1/4 cup crumbled goat cheese, 2 tbsp balsamic vinegar, 1 tbsp olive oil.
- **Procedure:** Toss arugula, beetroot slices, walnuts, and goat cheese in a bowl. Drizzle with balsamic vinegar and olive oil.
- **N.V.:** High in antioxidants, fiber, and healthy fats.
- **Suggestions:** Perfect for a light yet satisfying lunch, supporting liver health and digestion.

Kale and Avocado Liver Support Salad

- **P.T.:** 10 mins
- **Ingr.:** 2 cups kale (chopped and massaged), 1 ripe avocado (cubed), 1/2 cup cherry tomatoes, 2 tbsp pumpkin seeds, lemon vinaigrette dressing.
- **Procedure:** Combine kale, avocado, and cherry tomatoes. Top with pumpkin seeds and drizzle with lemon vinaigrette.
- **N.V.:** Rich in vitamins A, C, E, and healthy fats.
- **Suggestions:** Ideal for a nutrient-dense meal that aids in liver detoxification.

Quinoa and Edamame Liver Cleanse Bowl

- **P.T.:** 20 mins
- **Ingr.:** 1 cup cooked quinoa, 1/2 cup shelled edamame, 1 carrot (shredded), 1/4 cup sliced red cabbage, ginger dressing.
- **Procedure:** Mix quinoa, edamame, carrot, and red cabbage. Top with ginger dressing.
- **N.V.:** Provides a balanced mix of protein, fiber, and essential minerals.
- **Suggestions:** A filling and flavorful option for maintaining liver health.

Detoxifying Spinach and Apple Salad

- **P.T.:** 10 mins
- **Ingr.:** 2 cups baby spinach, 1 apple (sliced), 1/4 cup dried cranberries, 1/4 cup sliced almonds, apple cider vinaigrette.
- **Procedure:** Combine spinach, apple slices, cranberries, and almonds. Toss with apple cider vinaigrette.
- **N.V.:** High in dietary fiber, vitamin K, and antioxidants.
- **Suggestions:** A crisp, refreshing salad ideal for a midday liver cleanse.

Citrus and Walnut Liver-Boosting Salad

- **P.T.:** 12 mins
- **Ingr.:** Mixed greens, 1 orange (segmented), 1/4 cup walnuts, 1/4 cup feta cheese, orange-mustard dressing.
- **Procedure:** Arrange mixed greens on a plate, top with orange segments, walnuts, and feta cheese. Drizzle with orange-mustard dressing.
- **N.V.:** Rich in vitamin C, omega-3 fatty acids, and calcium.
- **Suggestions:** Enjoy this vibrant salad for its liver detoxifying benefits and delightful flavors.

Wholesome Soups and Stews for Liver Health

Miso Ginger Vegetable Soup

- **P.T.:** 25 mins
- **Ingr.:** 1 tbsp miso paste, 1/2 inch ginger (grated), 1 cup mixed vegetables (carrots, bok choy, mushrooms), 4 cups vegetable broth, 1 tbsp soy sauce, tofu cubes.
- **Procedure:** Dissolve miso paste in a bit of warm broth. Sauté ginger, add vegetables and tofu, pour in broth and soy sauce. Simmer until vegetables are tender. Stir in miso mixture before serving.
- **N.V.:** Rich in probiotics, antioxidants, and essential vitamins.
- **Suggestions:** Ideal for a light yet nourishing lunch, promoting liver health and digestion.

Turmeric Lentil Stew

- **P.T.:** 35 mins
- **Ingr.:** 1 cup red lentils, 1/2 tsp turmeric, 1 onion (chopped), 2 garlic cloves (minced), 4 cups vegetable broth, 1 can diced tomatoes, 1 tsp cumin.
- **Procedure:** Sauté onion and garlic. Add lentils, turmeric, cumin, broth, and tomatoes. Simmer until lentils are soft.
- **N.V.:** High in fiber, protein, and anti-inflammatory properties.
- **Suggestions:** A hearty, comforting stew perfect for supporting liver function.

Chicken and Kale Detox Broth

- **P.T.:** 40 mins
- **Ingr.:** 2 chicken breasts, 2 cups kale (chopped), 1 carrot (sliced), 1 onion (chopped), 4 cups chicken broth, 1 tsp thyme.
- **Procedure:** Cook chicken in broth with vegetables and thyme until fully cooked. Shred chicken and return to the soup.
- **N.V.:** Rich in protein, vitamins A and C, and minerals.
- **Suggestions:** A protein-packed soup that aids in liver detoxification and repair.

Spicy Tomato and Bean Soup

- **P.T.:** 30 mins
- **Ingr.:** 1 can diced tomatoes, 1 can kidney beans, 1 bell pepper (chopped), 1 onion (chopped), 1 jalapeño (minced), 4 cups vegetable broth, 1 tsp paprika.

- **Procedure:** Sauté onion, bell pepper, and jalapeño. Add tomatoes, beans, broth, and paprika. Simmer for 20 minutes.
- **N.V.:** High in antioxidants, fiber, and plant-based protein.
- **Suggestions:** A vibrant, spicy soup ideal for a liver-friendly lunch with a kick.

Butternut Squash and Ginger Soup

- **P.T.:** 45 mins
- **Ingr.:** 1 butternut squash (peeled and cubed), 1/2 inch ginger (grated), 1 onion (chopped), 4 cups vegetable broth, 1 tsp cinnamon.
- **Procedure:** Roast squash until tender. Sauté onion and ginger, add squash, broth, and cinnamon. Blend until smooth.
- **N.V.:** Loaded with vitamins A and C, and anti-inflammatory properties.
- **Suggestions:** A creamy, warming soup perfect for supporting liver health and boosting immunity.

Lean Protein Dishes for Liver Health

Grilled Turmeric Chicken

- **P.T.:** 30 mins
- **Ingr.:** 2 chicken breasts, 1 tsp turmeric, 1 garlic clove (minced), 1 tbsp olive oil, salt, and pepper to taste.
- **Procedure:** Marinate chicken with turmeric, garlic, olive oil, salt, and pepper. Grill until fully cooked.
- **N.V.:** High in protein, low in fat, and contains anti-inflammatory properties.
- **Suggestions:** Serve with a side of steamed vegetables for a complete meal.

Salmon with Dill and Lemon

- **P.T.:** 25 mins
- **Ingr.:** 2 salmon fillets, 1 tbsp fresh dill (chopped), 1 lemon (sliced), salt and pepper to taste.
- **Procedure:** Season salmon with salt, pepper, and dill. Place lemon slices on top. Bake until flaky.
- **N.V.:** Rich in omega-3 fatty acids and protein.
- **Suggestions:** Ideal for a heart-healthy lunch that supports liver function.

Tofu and Broccoli Stir-Fry

- **P.T.:** 20 mins
- **Ingr.:** 1 block firm tofu (cubed), 2 cups broccoli florets, 1 tbsp soy sauce, 1 tsp ginger (grated), 1 tbsp sesame oil.
- **Procedure:** Stir-fry tofu and broccoli in sesame oil. Add soy sauce and ginger. Cook until broccoli is tender.
- **N.V.:** High in plant-based protein and essential nutrients.
- **Suggestions:** A delicious vegan option that's both filling and liver-friendly.

Lemon Herb Grilled Shrimp

- **P.T.:** 15 mins
- **Ingr.:** 1 lb shrimp (peeled and deveined), 1 lemon (juiced), 1 tbsp mixed herbs (parsley, cilantro, dill), 1 garlic clove (minced), salt and pepper.
- **Procedure:** Marinate shrimp in lemon juice, herbs, garlic, salt, and pepper. Grill until pink and opaque.
- **N.V.:** Low in fat, high in protein and essential minerals.
- **Suggestions:** Serve over a bed of mixed greens for a light, nutritious meal.

Spiced Lentil Patty

- **P.T.:** 35 mins
- **Ingr.:** 1 cup cooked lentils, 1 onion (finely chopped), 1 carrot (grated), 1 tsp cumin, 1 tsp coriander, 2 tbsp whole wheat flour, salt and pepper to taste.
- **Procedure:** Mash lentils. Mix with onion, carrot, spices, flour, salt, and pepper. Form into patties and pan-fry until crisp.
- **N.V.:** High in fiber, plant-based protein, and vitamins.
- **Suggestions:** A great alternative to meat patties, perfect for a healthy, satisfying lunch.

Quick and Easy Lunch Ideas for Busy Days

Avocado Chickpea Salad Wrap

- **P.T.:** 10 mins
- **Ingr.:** 1 ripe avocado (mashed), 1/2 cup chickpeas, 1/4 cup diced red onion, 1 tbsp lemon juice, 2 whole grain wraps, salt and pepper to taste.
- **Procedure:** Mix avocado, chickpeas, red onion, and lemon juice. Season with salt and pepper. Spread on wraps and roll up.
- **N.V.:** Rich in healthy fats, protein, and fiber.
- **Suggestions:** A satisfying, no-cook option that's easy to pack and perfect for on-the-go lunches.

Zesty Quinoa Tabbouleh

- **P.T.:** 15 mins
- **Ingr.:** 1 cup cooked quinoa, 1/2 cup chopped parsley, 1/4 cup chopped mint, 1 diced tomato, 1 diced cucumber, 2 tbsp olive oil, lemon juice, salt and pepper.
- **Procedure:** Combine all ingredients in a bowl. Toss with olive oil and lemon juice. Season with salt and pepper.
- **N.V.:** High in antioxidants, vitamins, and minerals.
- **Suggestions:** A refreshing and light meal, great for a quick yet nutritious lunch.

Greek Yogurt and Berry Parfait

- **P.T.:** 5 mins
- **Ingr.:** 1 cup Greek yogurt, 1/2 cup mixed berries, 1/4 cup granola, 1 tbsp honey.
- **Procedure:** Layer Greek yogurt, berries, and granola in a glass. Drizzle with honey.
- **N.V.:** Packed with protein, probiotics, and antioxidants.
- **Suggestions:** An ideal quick lunch or snack, balancing sweetness with nutritional value.

Tuna and Avocado Lettuce Wraps

- **P.T.:** 10 mins
- **Ingr.:** 1 can tuna (drained), 1 ripe avocado (mashed), 1 tbsp chopped chives, 1 tbsp lemon juice, salt and pepper, lettuce leaves.
- **Procedure:** Mix tuna with avocado, chives, and lemon juice. Season with salt and pepper. Scoop into lettuce leaves and wrap.
- **N.V.:** High in omega-3 fatty acids and lean protein.
- **Suggestions:** A light, refreshing, and easy-to-assemble lunch, perfect for busy days.

Spicy Black Bean Bowl

- **P.T.:** 15 mins
- **Ingr.:** 1 cup cooked black beans, 1/2 cup corn, 1 diced bell pepper, 1/2 cup salsa, 1/4 cup shredded cheese, cilantro for garnish.
- **Procedure:** Mix black beans, corn, bell pepper, and salsa. Heat if desired. Top with cheese and cilantro.
- **N.V.:** Rich in fiber, protein, and essential nutrients.
- **Suggestions:** A hearty, flavorful bowl that's quick to prepare and packed with liver-friendly ingredients.

Chapter 5: Nourishing Dinner Recipes

Liver-Friendly Vegetarian Dishes

Stuffed Bell Peppers with Quinoa and Veggies

- **P.T.:** 40 mins
- **Ingr.:** 4 bell peppers, 1 cup cooked quinoa, 1/2 cup chopped mushrooms, 1/2 cup spinach, 1/4 cup diced onions, 1 clove garlic (minced), 1/2 cup tomato sauce, 1/4 cup shredded mozzarella, olive oil.
- **Procedure:** Sauté onions, garlic, mushrooms, and spinach. Mix in quinoa and tomato sauce. Stuff peppers with the mixture, top with cheese, and bake until tender.
- **N.V.:** High in fiber, vitamins, and minerals.
- **Suggestions:** A hearty, nutritious meal that is as visually appealing as it is delicious.

Curried Lentil and Sweet Potato Stew

- **P.T.:** 45 mins
- **Ingr.:** 1 cup red lentils, 1 large sweet potato (cubed), 1 onion (chopped), 2 cups vegetable broth, 1 tsp curry powder, 1/2 tsp turmeric, 1 can coconut milk.
- **Procedure:** Cook onion, sweet potato, spices, and lentils in broth until tender. Stir in coconut milk and simmer.
- **N.V.:** Rich in antioxidants, plant-based protein, and healthy fats.
- **Suggestions:** Perfect for a cozy, warming dinner, nourishing and supportive for liver health.

Eggplant and Chickpea Ratatouille

- **P.T.:** 50 mins
- **Ingr.:** 1 eggplant (cubed), 1 can chickpeas (drained), 1 zucchini (sliced), 1 bell pepper (chopped), 1 onion (chopped), 2 tomatoes (diced), 1 tbsp olive oil, herbs de Provence.
- **Procedure:** Sauté vegetables in olive oil, add tomatoes and herbs. Simmer until vegetables are tender. Add chickpeas last.
- **N.V.:** A great source of dietary fiber, vitamins, and plant-based protein.
- **Suggestions:** A colorful, nutrient-rich dish that's both filling and liver-friendly.

Spinach and Ricotta Stuffed Portobello Mushrooms

- **P.T.:** 30 mins
- **Ingr.:** 4 large portobello mushrooms, 1 cup ricotta cheese, 2 cups spinach, 1/4 cup grated Parmesan, 1 garlic clove (minced), salt and pepper.
- **Procedure:** Sauté spinach and garlic. Mix with ricotta, stuff into mushroom caps, sprinkle with Parmesan, and bake.
- **N.V.:** High in calcium, iron, and protein.
- **Suggestions:** An elegant and satisfying dish, ideal for a light yet fulfilling dinner.

Roasted Vegetable Buddha Bowl

- **P.T.:** 35 mins
- **Ingr.:** 1/2 cup quinoa, assorted vegetables (carrots, broccoli, bell peppers), 1 avocado (sliced), 1 tbsp tahini, lemon juice, olive oil, salt, and pepper.
- **Procedure:** Roast vegetables with olive oil, salt, and pepper. Cook quinoa. Arrange quinoa, vegetables, and avocado in a bowl, drizzle with tahini and lemon juice.
- **N.V.:** Packed with essential nutrients, healthy fats, and whole grains.
- **Suggestions:** A customizable, nutrient-dense bowl that's both visually appealing and beneficial for liver health.

Seafood and Lean Meat Options for Dinner

Herb-Crusted Salmon with Asparagus

- **P.T.:** 20 mins
- **Ingr.:** 2 salmon fillets, 1 bunch asparagus, 1 tbsp olive oil, 1 tsp mixed dried herbs (thyme, oregano, basil), lemon slices, salt, and pepper.
- **Procedure:** Brush salmon with olive oil, coat with herbs, season. Bake with asparagus and lemon slices until salmon is flaky.
- **N.V.:** Rich in omega-3 fatty acids, protein, and vitamins A, C.
- **Suggestions:** A simple, elegant dish that's perfect for supporting liver health and easy to prepare.

Grilled Chicken with Mediterranean Quinoa

- **P.T.:** 30 mins
- **Ingr.:** 2 chicken breasts, 1 cup quinoa, 1/2 cup cherry tomatoes, 1/4 cup olives, 1/4 cup feta cheese, olive oil, lemon juice, salt, and pepper.
- **Procedure:** Grill chicken until cooked. Prepare quinoa, mix in tomatoes, olives, and feta. Serve chicken over quinoa, drizzle with olive oil and lemon juice.
- **N.V.:** High in lean protein, fiber, and healthy fats.
- **Suggestions:** A balanced, nutritious meal that's satisfying and liver-friendly.

Spicy Shrimp and Veggie Stir-Fry

- **P.T.:** 25 mins
- **Ingr.:** 1 lb shrimp (peeled and deveined), mixed vegetables (bell peppers, broccoli, carrots), 2 tbsp soy sauce, 1 tsp chili flakes, 1 tbsp olive oil, garlic (minced).
- **Procedure:** Stir-fry shrimp and vegetables in olive oil and garlic. Add soy sauce and chili flakes. Cook until shrimp is pink and vegetables are tender.
- **N.V.:** Rich in protein, antioxidants, and vitamins.
- **Suggestions:** A quick and flavorful dish, great for a spicy twist on liver-friendly dinners.

Lemon Garlic Tilapia with Zucchini Noodles

- **P.T.:** 20 mins
- **Ingr.:** 2 tilapia fillets, 2 zucchinis (spiralized), 1 lemon (juiced), 2 garlic cloves (minced), 1 tbsp olive oil, parsley for garnish, salt, and pepper.
- **Procedure:** Sauté garlic in olive oil, add lemon juice. Cook tilapia in this mixture. Serve over zucchini noodles, garnished with parsley.
- **N.V.:** High in lean protein, low in carbohydrates, and rich in vitamin C.
- **Suggestions:** A light, refreshing meal that's perfect for a healthy, liver-supportive dinner.

Turkey and Vegetable Skewers

- **P.T.:** 30 mins
- **Ingr.:** 1 lb turkey breast (cut into cubes), bell peppers, onions, cherry tomatoes, 1 tbsp olive oil, mixed herbs (rosemary, thyme), salt, and pepper.
- **Procedure:** Thread turkey and vegetables onto skewers. Brush with olive oil and herbs. Grill until turkey is cooked.
- **N.V.:** A good source of lean protein and essential nutrients.
- **Suggestions:** An enjoyable, interactive dish that's both nutritious and fun to eat.

Whole Grain and Fiber-Rich Meals

Barley and Roasted Vegetable Medley

- **P.T.:** 40 mins
- **Ingr.:** 1 cup barley, 2 cups vegetable broth, 1 zucchini (cubed), 1 bell pepper (cubed), 1 red onion (chopped), 1 tbsp olive oil, mixed herbs (rosemary, thyme), salt, and pepper.
- **Procedure:** Cook barley in broth until tender. Roast vegetables with olive oil and herbs. Combine cooked barley and roasted vegetables.
- **N.V.:** High in fiber, B vitamins, and minerals.
- **Suggestions:** A hearty and satisfying meal, perfect for promoting digestive and liver health.

Farro and Mushroom Risotto

- **P.T.:** 45 mins
- **Ingr.:** 1 cup farro, 3 cups mushroom broth, 1 cup mushrooms (sliced), 1 onion (chopped), 2 garlic cloves (minced), 1/4 cup Parmesan cheese, 1 tbsp olive oil, parsley for garnish.
- **Procedure:** Sauté onion, garlic, and mushrooms. Add farro and broth, simmer until farro is creamy. Stir in Parmesan and garnish with parsley.
- **N.V.:** Rich in antioxidants, fiber, and protein.
- **Suggestions:** A luxurious dish that's both comforting and liver-friendly.

Bulgur Wheat and Lentil Pilaf

- **P.T.:** 30 mins
- **Ingr.:** 1 cup bulgur wheat, 1/2 cup lentils, 1 carrot (diced), 1 onion (diced), 2 cups vegetable broth, 1 tsp cumin, olive oil, salt, and pepper.
- **Procedure:** Cook lentils and bulgur in broth with onion, carrot, and cumin. Season to taste.
- **N.V.:** High in plant-based protein, fiber, and iron.
- **Suggestions:** A filling meal that supports liver function and provides sustained energy.

Quinoa Stuffed Acorn Squash

- **P.T.:** 50 mins
- **Ingr.:** 2 acorn squash (halved and seeded), 1 cup quinoa, 2 cups vegetable broth, 1/4 cup dried cranberries, 1/4 cup chopped walnuts, 1 tsp cinnamon, olive oil, salt, and pepper.
- **Procedure:** Roast squash halves until tender. Cook quinoa in broth with cinnamon. Mix in cranberries and walnuts. Stuff squash with quinoa mixture.
- **N.V.:** Rich in omega-3 fatty acids, antioxidants, and complex carbs.
- **Suggestions:** A visually stunning and nutritious dish, ideal for a wholesome dinner.

Whole Wheat Pasta with Kale and Pine Nuts

- **P.T.:** 20 mins
- **Ingr.:** 1/2 lb whole wheat pasta, 2 cups kale (chopped), 1/4 cup pine nuts, 1 garlic clove (minced), 1 lemon (zested and juiced), olive oil, salt, and pepper.
- **Procedure:** Cook pasta. Sauté kale, pine nuts, and garlic. Combine with pasta, lemon zest, and juice.
- **N.V.:** A great source of fiber, vitamin C, and healthy fats.
- **Suggestions:** A light yet fulfilling meal, perfect for maintaining a healthy liver.

Light and Healthy Dinner Ideas

Zesty Lime Shrimp Zoodle Bowl

- **P.T.:** 20 mins
- **Ingr.:** 1 lb shrimp (peeled and deveined), 2 large zucchinis (spiralized), 1 lime (juiced and zested), 1 garlic clove (minced), 1 tbsp olive oil, cilantro for garnish, chili flakes, salt, and pepper.
- **Procedure:** Sauté shrimp with garlic, lime juice, and zest in olive oil. Toss with zoodles, garnish with cilantro and chili flakes.
- **N.V.:** Rich in protein, vitamin C, and low in carbohydrates.
- **Suggestions:** A refreshing and light meal, perfect for a satisfying yet liver-friendly dinner.

Grilled Chicken and Avocado Salad

- **P.T.:** 25 mins
- **Ingr.:** 2 chicken breasts, mixed salad greens, 1 ripe avocado (sliced), cherry tomatoes, cucumber slices, balsamic vinaigrette, salt, and pepper.
- **Procedure:** Grill chicken, season with salt and pepper. Toss greens, avocado, tomatoes, and cucumber. Top with sliced chicken, drizzle with vinaigrette.
- **N.V.:** High in lean protein, healthy fats, and antioxidants.
- **Suggestions:** A balanced and nourishing salad that's both fulfilling and light.

Soy-Glazed Salmon with Steamed Greens

- **P.T.:** 30 mins
- **Ingr.:** 2 salmon fillets, 2 tbsp soy sauce, 1 tsp honey, 1 tsp ginger (grated), mixed greens (spinach, kale), 1 tbsp sesame seeds.
- **Procedure:** Marinate salmon in soy sauce, honey, and ginger. Grill until cooked. Steam greens, top with salmon, sprinkle sesame seeds.
- **N.V.:** Rich in omega-3 fatty acids, vitamins, and minerals.
- **Suggestions:** An easy-to-make, flavorful dish that supports liver health.

Chickpea and Vegetable Stir-Fry

- **P.T.:** 20 mins
- **Ingr.:** 1 can chickpeas (drained), mixed vegetables (bell pepper, broccoli, carrot), 1 tbsp olive oil, 2 tbsp soy sauce, 1 garlic clove (minced), 1 tsp sesame oil.
- **Procedure:** Sauté vegetables and chickpeas in olive oil and garlic. Add soy sauce and sesame oil. Cook until veggies are tender.
- **N.V.:** High in plant-based protein, fiber, and essential nutrients.
- **Suggestions:** A quick, vegan-friendly meal that's both hearty and healthy.

Roasted Cauliflower Steaks with Tahini Drizzle

- **P.T.:** 35 mins
- **Ingr.:** 2 large cauliflower heads (sliced into 'steaks'), 2 tbsp olive oil, salt and pepper, 2 tbsp tahini, lemon juice, parsley for garnish.
- **Procedure:** Brush cauliflower steaks with olive oil, season with salt and pepper. Roast until tender. Drizzle with tahini and lemon juice, garnish with parsley.
- **N.V.:** Low in calories, high in fiber, and rich in antioxidants.
- **Suggestions:** A flavorful, plant-based dish that's perfect for a light yet satisfying dinner.

Chapter 6: Snacks and Small Bites

Nutritious Snack Ideas

Spiced Chickpea Crunch

- **P.T.:** 30 mins
- **Ingr.:** 1 can chickpeas (drained and dried), 1 tbsp olive oil, 1/2 tsp paprika, 1/4 tsp cumin, salt, and pepper.
- **Procedure:** Toss chickpeas with oil, spices, salt, and pepper. Roast until crispy.
- **N.V.:** High in protein, fiber, and micronutrients.
- **Suggestions:** A savory, crunchy snack that's perfect for on-the-go or as a healthy alternative to chips.

Kale Chips with Nutritional Yeast

- **P.T.:** 20 mins
- **Ingr.:** 2 cups kale (torn into bite-sized pieces), 1 tbsp olive oil, 2 tbsp nutritional yeast, salt.
- **Procedure:** Toss kale with olive oil, nutritional yeast, and salt. Bake until crisp.
- **N.V.:** Rich in vitamins A, C, and K, plus added benefits of nutritional yeast.
- **Suggestions:** An excellent, crunchy snack that's both nutritious and delicious.

Carrot and Hummus Roll-Ups

- **P.T.:** 10 mins
- **Ingr.:** 1 large carrot (peeled into ribbons), 1/4 cup hummus, 1 tbsp sesame seeds, parsley for garnish.
- **Procedure:** Spread hummus on carrot ribbons, roll up, sprinkle with sesame seeds and parsley.
- **N.V.:** High in fiber, beta-carotene, and plant protein.
- **Suggestions:** A fresh, light snack ideal for a quick nutrient boost.

Apple Slices with Almond Butter

- **P.T.:** 5 mins
- **Ingr.:** 1 apple (sliced), 2 tbsp almond butter, cinnamon.
- **Procedure:** Spread almond butter on apple slices, sprinkle with cinnamon.
- **N.V.:** Good source of healthy fats, fiber, and vitamin C.
- **Suggestions:** A sweet and satisfying snack, perfect for midday cravings.

Avocado and Tomato Rice Cakes

- **P.T.:** 10 mins
- **Ingr.:** 2 rice cakes, 1 ripe avocado (mashed), 1 tomato (sliced), salt and pepper, lemon juice.
- **Procedure:** Top rice cakes with mashed avocado, tomato slices, season with salt, pepper, and a squeeze of lemon juice.
- **N.V.:** Rich in healthy fats, lycopene, and whole grains.
- **Suggestions:** A quick and healthy snack that's both filling and flavorful.

Healthy Dips and Spreads

Creamy Avocado and Cilantro Dip

- **P.T.:** 10 mins
- **Ingr.:** 2 ripe avocados, 1/4 cup fresh cilantro, 1 lime (juiced), 1 garlic clove, salt and pepper to taste.
- **Procedure:** Blend avocados, cilantro, lime juice, and garlic until smooth. Season with salt and pepper.
- **N.V.:** High in healthy fats, vitamin E, and antioxidants.
- **Suggestions:** Perfect as a dip for raw veggies or a spread for whole grain crackers.

Roasted Red Pepper Hummus

- **P.T.:** 15 mins
- **Ingr.:** 1 can chickpeas (drained), 1 roasted red pepper, 2 tbsp tahini, 1 lemon (juiced), 1 garlic clove, olive oil, cumin, salt, and pepper.
- **Procedure:** Process all ingredients until smooth, drizzle with olive oil.
- **N.V.:** Rich in protein, fiber, and vitamin C.
- **Suggestions:** A flavorful, liver-friendly spread for sandwiches or a dip for pita bread.

Spicy Black Bean Dip

- **P.T.:** 20 mins
- **Ingr.:** 1 can black beans (drained), 1/2 onion (chopped), 1 tomato (chopped), 1 jalapeño (minced), 1 lime (juiced), cilantro, cumin, salt, and pepper.
- **Procedure:** Sauté onion and jalapeño, blend with beans, tomato, lime juice, and spices.
- **N.V.:** High in plant-based protein and fiber.
- **Suggestions:** A robust dip that pairs well with corn tortilla chips or veggie sticks.

Sun-dried Tomato and Basil Pesto

- **P.T.:** 15 mins
- **Ingr.:** 1/2 cup sun-dried tomatoes, 1/4 cup basil leaves, 1/4 cup Parmesan cheese, 1/4 cup pine nuts, olive oil, garlic, salt, and pepper.
- **Procedure:** Blend all ingredients, adding olive oil gradually until desired consistency is reached.
- **N.V.:** Contains healthy fats, lycopene, and antioxidants.
- **Suggestions:** Great as a pasta sauce or a spread for bruschetta.

Green Pea and Mint Spread

- **P.T.:** 10 mins
- **Ingr.:** 1 cup green peas (cooked and cooled), 1/4 cup mint leaves, 1 lemon (juiced), 1 garlic clove, olive oil, salt, and pepper.
- **Procedure:** Puree peas, mint, lemon juice, and garlic, drizzle with olive oil for smoothness.
- **N.V.:** Rich in vitamins A and C, and fiber.
- **Suggestions:** A refreshing and light spread for toast or as a dip for vegetable crudité.

Liver-Boosting Nuts and Seeds

Turmeric Spiced Walnuts

- **P.T.:** 15 mins
- **Ingr.:** 1 cup walnuts, 1 tsp turmeric powder, 1/2 tsp cayenne pepper, salt, 1 tbsp olive oil.
- **Procedure:** Toss walnuts with olive oil, turmeric, cayenne, and salt. Bake until toasted.
- **N.V.:** High in omega-3 fatty acids, antioxidants.
- **Suggestions:** A perfect snack for liver health, combining the benefits of walnuts with the anti-inflammatory properties of turmeric.

Cinnamon Roasted Almonds

- **P.T.:** 20 mins
- **Ingr.:** 1 cup almonds, 2 tbsp honey, 1 tsp cinnamon, a pinch of salt.
- **Procedure:** Mix almonds with honey, cinnamon, and salt. Roast until crunchy.
- **N.V.:** Rich in healthy fats, vitamin E.
- **Suggestions:** A sweet, satisfying snack that's beneficial for liver health and easy to make.

Sesame and Flax Seed Crackers

- **P.T.:** 30 mins
- **Ingr.:** 1/2 cup ground flax seeds, 1/2 cup sesame seeds, 1 cup water, salt, and pepper.
- **Procedure:** Combine all ingredients, spread thinly on a baking sheet. Bake until crisp.
- **N.V.:** High in fiber, omega-3 fatty acids.
- **Suggestions:** Pair these crackers with a healthy dip for a nutrient-dense snack.

Chia and Pumpkin Seed Trail Mix

- **P.T.:** 10 mins
- **Ingr.:** 1/2 cup chia seeds, 1/2 cup pumpkin seeds, 1/2 cup dried cranberries, 1/2 cup unsweetened coconut flakes.
- **Procedure:** Mix all ingredients in a bowl.
- **N.V.:** Loaded with fiber, protein, and essential minerals.
- **Suggestions:** A great on-the-go snack, ideal for a quick liver health boost.

Honey-Glazed Pecans with Sea Salt

- **P.T.:** 15 mins
- **Ingr.:** 1 cup pecans, 2 tbsp honey, a pinch of sea salt.

- **Procedure:** Toss pecans with honey, bake until golden, sprinkle with sea salt.
- **N.V.:** Contains healthy fats, magnesium, and zinc.
- **Suggestions:** A delightful treat that's both sweet and salty, perfect for a healthy snack option.

Fruit-Based Snacks

Mango and Chia Seed Pudding

- **P.T.:** Overnight + 10 mins
- **Ingr.:** 1 ripe mango (pureed), 1/4 cup chia seeds, 1 cup coconut milk, 1 tsp honey, a pinch of ground ginger.
- **Procedure:** Mix chia seeds with coconut milk, honey, and ginger. Refrigerate overnight. Layer with mango puree before serving.

- **N.V.:** Rich in omega-3 fatty acids, fiber, and vitamin C.
- **Suggestions:** A tropical, refreshing snack that's perfect for a liver-healthy diet.

Baked Cinnamon Apple Chips

- **P.T.:** 45 mins
- **Ingr.:** 2 apples (thinly sliced), 1 tsp cinnamon, a sprinkle of nutmeg.
- **Procedure:** Arrange apple slices on a baking sheet, sprinkle with cinnamon and nutmeg. Bake until crisp.
- **N.V.:** High in fiber and low in calories.
- **Suggestions:** A crunchy, naturally sweet treat, great for satisfying sugar cravings healthily.

Frozen Berry Yogurt Bites

- **P.T.:** 1 hr
- **Ingr.:** 1 cup Greek yogurt, 1/2 cup mixed berries (chopped), 1 tbsp honey.
- **Procedure:** Mix yogurt with honey, fold in berries. Spoon into mini muffin cups and freeze.
- **N.V.:** Packed with protein, antioxidants, and probiotics.
- **Suggestions:** A delightful, bite-sized snack perfect for a hot day or a quick dessert.

Pineapple and Cottage Cheese Bowl

- **P.T.:** 5 mins
- **Ingr.:** 1/2 cup cottage cheese, 1/2 cup pineapple (chopped), 1 tbsp shredded coconut, 1 tsp honey.
- **Procedure:** Combine cottage cheese with pineapple, top with coconut and honey.
- **N.V.:** Rich in protein, vitamin C, and digestive enzymes.
- **Suggestions:** An easy and nutritious snack, balancing sweetness with protein.

Kiwi and Pomegranate Salad

- **P.T.:** 10 mins
- **Ingr.:** 2 kiwis (peeled and sliced), 1/2 cup pomegranate seeds, a squeeze of fresh lime juice, mint leaves for garnish.
- **Procedure:** Mix kiwi and pomegranate seeds, drizzle with lime juice. Garnish with mint leaves.

- **N.V.:** High in vitamins, antioxidants, and fiber.
- **Suggestions:** A vibrant, refreshing snack, perfect for an afternoon pick-me-up.

Chapter 7: Healthy Fats and Oils

Cooking with Liver-Friendly Oils

Grilled Zucchini with Flaxseed Oil Dressing

- **P.T.:** 20 mins
- **Ingr.:** 2 large zucchinis (sliced), 2 tbsp flaxseed oil, 1 tbsp apple cider vinegar, 1 tsp Dijon mustard, garlic powder, salt, pepper.
- **Procedure:** Grill zucchini slices. Whisk together flaxseed oil, vinegar, mustard, garlic powder, salt, and pepper for dressing. Drizzle over grilled zucchini.
- **N.V.:** High in ALA (alpha-linolenic acid), low in saturated fats.
- **Suggestions:** Serve as a side dish or add to salads.

Turmeric and Walnut Roasted Cauliflower

- **P.T.:** 35 mins
- **Ingr.:** 1 head cauliflower (cut into florets), 2 tbsp walnut oil, 1 tsp ground turmeric, cumin seeds, salt.
- **Procedure:** Toss cauliflower with walnut oil, turmeric, cumin seeds, and salt. Roast at 400°F until tender.
- **N.V.:** Rich in omega-3 fatty acids and antioxidants.
- **Suggestions:** Pair with quinoa or brown rice for a complete meal.

Avocado Pesto Pasta

- **P.T.:** 25 mins
- **Ingr.:** Whole grain pasta (200g), 1 ripe avocado, fresh basil leaves, 2 cloves garlic, 2 tbsp olive oil, lemon juice, pine nuts, salt.
- **Procedure:** Cook pasta. Blend avocado, basil, garlic, olive oil, lemon juice, pine nuts, and salt for pesto. Toss with pasta.
- **N.V.:** High in healthy monounsaturated fats, fiber.
- **Suggestions:** Top with cherry tomatoes and extra pine nuts.

Chia and Hemp Seed Oatmeal

- **P.T.:** 15 mins
- **Ingr.:** Rolled oats (1 cup), 2 tbsp chia seeds, 2 tbsp hemp seeds, almond milk (2 cups), cinnamon, vanilla extract.
- **Procedure:** Cook oats with almond milk, chia seeds, hemp seeds, cinnamon, and vanilla.
- **N.V.:** Source of omega-3 and omega-6 fatty acids, high in protein.
- **Suggestions:** Serve with fresh berries or a drizzle of honey.

Spiced Salmon with Almond Crust

- **P.T.:** 30 mins
- **Ingr.:** 4 salmon fillets, 1/2 cup ground almonds, paprika, garlic powder, olive oil, lemon zest, salt, pepper.
- **Procedure:** Mix almonds, paprika, garlic powder, lemon zest, salt, and pepper. Coat salmon with olive oil, press almond mixture onto fillets. Bake at 350°F.
- **N.V.:** Rich in omega-3 fatty acids, essential vitamins.
- **Suggestions:** Accompany with a side of steamed greens or a fresh salad.

Homemade Dressings and Sauces

Sesame Ginger Dressing

- **P.T.:** 10 mins
- **Ingr.:** 2 tbsp toasted sesame oil, 2 tbsp rice vinegar, 1 tbsp fresh ginger (grated), 1 tsp soy sauce (low sodium), 1 tsp honey, 1 clove garlic (minced).
- **Procedure:** Whisk together all ingredients until well combined.
- **N.V.:** Rich in healthy fats, low in sugar.
- **Suggestions:** Ideal for dressing Asian-style salads or drizzling over steamed vegetables.

Avocado Cilantro Lime Sauce

- **P.T.:** 15 mins
- **Ingr.:** 1 ripe avocado, 1/4 cup cilantro leaves, 2 tbsp lime juice, 1 clove garlic, 2 tbsp Greek yogurt, water (as needed), salt, pepper.
- **Procedure:** Blend avocado, cilantro, lime juice, garlic, yogurt, and water until smooth. Season with salt and pepper.
- **N.V.:** High in monounsaturated fats, vitamins.
- **Suggestions:** Use as a dip for veggies or a creamy sauce for tacos.

Walnut Pesto

- **P.T.:** 10 mins
- **Ingr.:** 1/2 cup walnuts, 2 cups fresh basil leaves, 1/2 cup Parmesan cheese, 2 cloves garlic, 1/2 cup olive oil, salt, pepper.
- **Procedure:** Pulse walnuts, basil, Parmesan, and garlic in a food processor. Gradually add olive oil until smooth. Season with salt and pepper.
- **N.V.:** Source of omega-3 fatty acids and antioxidants.
- **Suggestions:** Perfect for pasta dishes or as a spread for sandwiches.

Lemon Tahini Dressing

- **P.T.:** 10 mins
- **Ingr.:** 1/4 cup tahini, 1/4 cup lemon juice, 2 tbsp water, 1 tbsp olive oil, 1 clove garlic (minced), salt, pepper.
- **Procedure:** Whisk together tahini, lemon juice, water, olive oil, and garlic. Add salt and pepper to taste.
- **N.V.:** Rich in healthy fats and minerals.
- **Suggestions:** Drizzle over roasted vegetables or grain bowls.

Spicy Almond Butter Sauce

- **P.T.:** 15 mins
- **Ingr.:** 1/4 cup almond butter, 2 tbsp soy sauce (low sodium), 1 tbsp lime juice, 1 tsp honey, 1 tsp chili flakes, warm water (as needed).
- **Procedure:** Mix almond butter, soy sauce, lime juice, honey, and chili flakes. Add warm water to reach desired consistency.
- **N.V.:** High in protein and healthy fats.
- **Suggestions:** Serve as a dipping sauce for spring rolls or drizzle over stir-fry dishes.

Incorporating Healthy Fats into Meals

Grilled Chicken with Avocado Salsa

- **P.T.:** 30 mins
- **Ingr.:** 4 chicken breasts, 2 avocados (diced), 1 tomato (diced), 1/4 cup red onion (chopped), 2 tbsp lime juice, 1 tbsp olive oil, cilantro, salt, pepper.
- **Procedure:** Grill chicken breasts until cooked. Mix avocados, tomato, onion, lime juice, olive oil, cilantro, salt, and pepper to make salsa. Serve over chicken.
- **N.V.:** High in protein and monounsaturated fats.
- **Suggestions:** Pair with a quinoa salad for a fulfilling meal.

Olive Oil Poached Salmon

- **P.T.:** 40 mins
- **Ingr.:** 4 salmon fillets, 2 cups olive oil, lemon slices, fresh herbs (dill, parsley), garlic cloves, salt, pepper.
- **Procedure:** Submerge salmon in a pot with olive oil, lemon, herbs, and garlic. Poach on low heat until salmon is tender.
- **N.V.:** Rich in omega-3 fatty acids.
- **Suggestions:** Serve with steamed vegetables or a light salad.

Roasted Nuts and Seeds Trail Mix

- **P.T.:** 20 mins
- **Ingr.:** 1/2 cup almonds, 1/2 cup walnuts, 1/4 cup pumpkin seeds, 1/4 cup sunflower seeds, 1 tbsp coconut oil, sea salt, chili powder.
- **Procedure:** Toss nuts and seeds with coconut oil, salt, and chili powder. Roast in oven until golden.
- **N.V.:** Source of healthy fats and protein.
- **Suggestions:** A great snack option, perfect for on-the-go energy.

Flaxseed Crusted Cod

- **P.T.:** 25 mins
- **Ingr.:** 4 cod fillets, 1/2 cup ground flaxseed, lemon zest, garlic powder, olive oil, salt, pepper.
- **Procedure:** Mix flaxseed, lemon zest, garlic powder, salt, and pepper. Coat cod with olive oil, then crust with flaxseed mix. Bake until flaky.
- **N.V.:** High in omega-3 fatty acids and low in carbs.
- **Suggestions:** Accompany with a kale and avocado salad.

Chia Seed and Berry Parfait

- **P.T.:** Overnight (prep time 10 mins)
- **Ingr.:** 3 tbsp chia seeds, 1 cup almond milk, 1 tbsp honey, mixed berries, Greek yogurt.
- **Procedure:** Mix chia seeds, almond milk, and honey. Refrigerate overnight. Layer with Greek yogurt and berries to serve.
- **N.V.:** High in omega-3s, fiber, and antioxidants.
- **Suggestions:** Ideal for a nutritious breakfast or dessert option.

Chapter 8: Detoxifying Drinks and Beverages

Herbal Teas for Liver Health

Milk Thistle and Peppermint Tea

- **P.T.:** 10 mins
- **Ingr.:** 1 tsp milk thistle seeds (crushed), 1 tsp peppermint leaves, 2 cups boiling water.
- **Procedure:** Steep milk thistle and peppermint in boiling water for 7 mins. Strain and serve.
- **N.V.:** Aids in liver health, soothes digestion.
- **Suggestions:** Enjoy after meals to enhance digestion.

Turmeric and Ginger Liver Tonic

- **P.T.:** 20 mins
- **Ingr.:** 1 tsp turmeric powder, 1/2 tsp ginger (grated), lemon juice (from 1/2 lemon), 2 cups water, honey (to taste).
- **Procedure:** Boil water, add turmeric and ginger. Simmer for 15 mins, add lemon juice, strain, and sweeten with honey.
- **N.V.:** Anti-inflammatory properties, supports liver function.
- **Suggestions:** Ideal as an evening drink to promote liver health.

Green Tea and Hibiscus Blend

- **P.T.:** 10 mins
- **Ingr.:** 1 green tea bag, 1 tsp dried hibiscus flowers, 2 cups hot water, honey (optional).
- **Procedure:** Steep green tea and hibiscus in hot water for 5 mins. Remove tea bag, strain hibiscus, and add honey if desired.
- **N.V.:** Rich in antioxidants, promotes liver health.
- **Suggestions:** A refreshing beverage, best enjoyed in the afternoon.

Licorice Root and Cinnamon Infusion

- **P.T.:** 15 mins
- **Ingr.:** 1 tsp licorice root, 1 cinnamon stick, 2 cups water, honey (optional).
- **Procedure:** Boil licorice root and cinnamon in water for 10 mins. Strain and add honey to taste.
- **N.V.:** Supports liver function, aids in detoxification.
- **Suggestions:** Suitable as a warming drink during cooler weather.

Homemade Detox Drinks

Beetroot and Lemon Cleanser

- **P.T.:** 10 mins
- **Ingr.:** 1 medium beetroot (peeled, diced), juice of 1 lemon, 1 tbsp grated ginger, 2 cups water, honey (optional).
- **Procedure:** Blend beetroot, lemon juice, and ginger with water. Strain and sweeten with honey if desired.
- **N.V.:** Rich in liver-cleansing compounds, antioxidants.
- **Suggestions:** Drink on an empty stomach for maximum detox benefits.

Cucumber and Mint Refresher

- **P.T.:** 5 mins
- **Ingr.:** 1 large cucumber, a handful of fresh mint leaves, juice of 1 lime, 2 cups water.
- **Procedure:** Blend cucumber, mint, and lime juice with water. Strain and serve chilled.
- **N.V.:** Hydrating, rich in liver-supporting nutrients.
- **Suggestions:** A perfect drink to hydrate and detoxify throughout the day.

Apple Cider Vinegar Tonic

- **P.T.:** 5 mins
- **Ingr.:** 2 tbsp apple cider vinegar, 1 tbsp lemon juice, 1 tsp honey, a pinch of cayenne pepper, 1 cup warm water.
- **Procedure:** Mix all ingredients in warm water until well combined.
- **N.V.:** Aids in detoxification and digestion.
- **Suggestions:** Consume in the morning to stimulate the liver.

Golden Turmeric Detox Drink

- **P.T.:** 10 mins
- **Ingr.:** 1/2 tsp turmeric powder, 1/2 tsp ginger powder, juice of 1/2 lemon, 1 tsp honey, 1 cup hot water.
- **Procedure:** Stir turmeric, ginger, lemon juice, and honey into hot water until dissolved.
- **N.V.:** Anti-inflammatory, supports liver function.
- **Suggestions:** Ideal for evenings; helps with detoxification and relaxation.

Pineapple and Parsley Flush

- **P.T.:** 10 mins
- **Ingr.:** 2 cups pineapple chunks, 1/4 cup parsley leaves, 1 tbsp chia seeds, 2 cups water.
- **Procedure:** Blend pineapple, parsley, and chia seeds with water. Strain and serve.
- **N.V.:** High in enzymes and antioxidants beneficial for liver health.
- **Suggestions:** A refreshing and cleansing drink, perfect for midday rejuvenation.

Chapter 9: Vegetarian and Vegan Options

Plant-Based Protein Sources

Quinoa and Black Bean Salad

- **P.T.:** 30 mins
- **Ingr.:** 1 cup quinoa, 1 can black beans (drained, rinsed), 1 red bell pepper (diced), 1/4 cup fresh cilantro (chopped), 2 tbsp lime juice, 1 tbsp olive oil, 1 tsp cumin, salt, pepper.
- **Procedure:** Cook quinoa as per instructions. Mix with black beans, bell pepper, cilantro. Whisk together lime juice, olive oil, cumin, salt, pepper, and dress the salad.
- **N.V.:** High in plant-based protein and fiber.
- **Suggestions:** Serve cold as a refreshing and filling salad.

Lentil and Spinach Stew

- **P.T.:** 45 mins
- **Ingr.:** 1 cup lentils, 2 cups spinach, 1 onion (chopped), 2 cloves garlic (minced), 1 can diced tomatoes, 1 tsp turmeric, 1 tsp cumin, vegetable broth, salt, pepper.
- **Procedure:** Sauté onion, garlic. Add lentils, tomatoes, spices, and broth. Simmer until lentils are tender. Stir in spinach until wilted.
- **N.V.:** Rich in protein, iron, and essential nutrients.
- **Suggestions:** Ideal for a hearty dinner; serve with whole-grain bread.

Tofu Scramble with Veggies

- **P.T.:** 20 mins
- **Ingr.:** 1 block firm tofu (crumbled), 1 bell pepper (diced), 1/2 onion (chopped), 1 cup spinach, 1 tsp turmeric, nutritional yeast, olive oil, salt, pepper.
- **Procedure:** Sauté onion, bell pepper. Add tofu, turmeric, nutritional yeast, salt, pepper. Cook until tofu is golden. Add spinach, cook until wilted.
- **N.V.:** High in protein and vitamins.
- **Suggestions:** A fulfilling breakfast option, can be served with avocado toast.

Chickpea and Sweet Potato Curry

- **P.T.:** 40 mins
- **Ingr.:** 1 can chickpeas (drained, rinsed), 1 sweet potato (cubed), 1 onion (chopped), 2 cloves garlic (minced), 1 can coconut milk, 1 tbsp curry powder, olive oil, salt, cilantro.
- **Procedure:** Sauté onion, garlic. Add sweet potato, chickpeas, curry powder, coconut milk. Simmer until sweet potatoes are tender. Garnish with cilantro.
- **N.V.:** Source of protein, healthy fats, and fiber.
- **Suggestions:** Serve with brown rice or quinoa for a complete meal.

Edamame and Avocado Spread

- **P.T.:** 15 mins
- **Ingr.:** 1 cup edamame (cooked), 1 ripe avocado, 1 lemon (juiced), 2 tbsp olive oil, garlic powder, salt, pepper.
- **Procedure:** Blend edamame, avocado, lemon juice, olive oil, garlic powder, salt, and pepper until smooth.
- **N.V.:** Rich in protein, healthy fats, and omega-3 fatty acids.
- **Suggestions:** Use as a spread on whole-grain toast or as a dip for vegetables.

Vegan Breakfast Ideas

Almond Butter and Banana Oatmeal

- **P.T.:** 15 mins
- **Ingr.:** 1 cup rolled oats, 2 cups almond milk, 1 ripe banana (mashed), 2 tbsp almond butter, 1 tsp cinnamon, a pinch of salt, maple syrup (optional).
- **Procedure:** Cook oats in almond milk with mashed banana, cinnamon, and salt. Once cooked, stir in almond butter. Sweeten with maple syrup if desired.
- **N.V.:** High in fiber, healthy fats, and plant protein.
- **Suggestions:** Top with sliced banana and a sprinkle of chia seeds for extra nutrition.

Vegan Berry Smoothie Bowl

- **P.T.:** 10 mins
- **Ingr.:** 1 cup mixed berries (frozen), 1 banana, 1/2 cup coconut yogurt, 1 tbsp flaxseeds, almond milk (as needed), toppings: granola, nuts, additional berries.
- **Procedure:** Blend berries, banana, yogurt, and flaxseeds, adding almond milk to achieve desired consistency. Pour into a bowl and add toppings.
- **N.V.:** Rich in vitamins, antioxidants, and omega-3 fatty acids.
- **Suggestions:** Customize with your favorite toppings for a nutritious start.

Avocado Toast with Tomato and Seeds

- **P.T.:** 10 mins
- **Ingr.:** 2 slices whole grain bread, 1 ripe avocado, 1 tomato (sliced), pumpkin seeds, sunflower seeds, lemon juice, salt, pepper.
- **Procedure:** Toast bread slices. Mash avocado with lemon juice, salt, and pepper. Spread on toast, top with tomato slices and a sprinkle of seeds.
- **N.V.:** Good source of healthy fats, fiber, and protein.
- **Suggestions:** Ideal for a quick, nutritious breakfast or snack.

Chia and Hemp Seed Pudding

- **P.T.:** Overnight (prep time 5 mins)
- **Ingr.:** 3 tbsp chia seeds, 2 tbsp hemp seeds, 1 cup almond milk, 1 tbsp maple syrup, 1/2 tsp vanilla extract.
- **Procedure:** Mix chia seeds, hemp seeds, almond milk, maple syrup, and vanilla in a bowl. Refrigerate overnight until set.
- **N.V.:** High in omega-3 fatty acids, protein, and fiber.
- **Suggestions:** Serve with fresh fruit or a dollop of coconut yogurt.

Tofu and Vegetable Scramble

- **P.T.:** 20 mins
- **Ingr.:** 1 block firm tofu (crumbled), 1/2 bell pepper (diced), 1/2 onion (diced), 1 cup spinach, 1 tsp turmeric, nutritional yeast, olive oil, salt, pepper.
- **Procedure:** Sauté onion and bell pepper in olive oil. Add tofu, turmeric, nutritional yeast, salt, and pepper. Cook until golden, then stir in spinach.
- **N.V.:** Rich in plant-based protein, vitamins, and minerals.
- **Suggestions:** Serve with whole-grain toast or wrapped in a tortilla for a breakfast burrito.

Hearty Vegetarian Dinners

Eggplant Chickpea Tagine

- **P.T.:** 45 mins
- **Ingr.:** 1 large eggplant (cubed), 1 can chickpeas (drained), 1 onion (chopped), 2 cloves garlic (minced), 1 can diced tomatoes, 1 tsp cumin, 1 tsp paprika, 1/2 tsp cinnamon, olive oil, salt, cilantro.
- **Procedure:** Sauté onion, garlic in olive oil. Add spices, eggplant, chickpeas, tomatoes. Simmer until eggplant is tender. Garnish with cilantro.
- **N.V.:** High in fiber, plant protein, and antioxidants.
- **Suggestions:** Serve with couscous or quinoa.

Stuffed Bell Peppers with Quinoa and Black Beans

- **P.T.:** 1 hr
- **Ingr.:** 4 bell peppers (halved, seeded), 1 cup quinoa (cooked), 1 can black beans (rinsed), 1 cup corn, 1/2 cup tomato sauce, cumin, garlic powder, olive oil, salt, pepper, shredded vegan cheese.
- **Procedure:** Mix quinoa, black beans, corn, tomato sauce, cumin, garlic powder, salt, and pepper. Stuff peppers, top with cheese. Bake at 350°F until peppers are tender.
- **N.V.:** Rich in vitamins, minerals, and protein.
- **Suggestions:** A colorful and nutritious main course.

Mushroom and Lentil Bolognese

- **P.T.:** 50 mins
- **Ingr.:** 1 cup green lentils, 2 cups mushrooms (chopped), 1 onion (chopped), 2 cloves garlic (minced), 1 can crushed tomatoes, 1 tsp oregano, basil, olive oil, salt, pepper, whole wheat pasta.
- **Procedure:** Cook lentils. Sauté onion, garlic, mushrooms in olive oil. Add tomatoes, herbs, cooked lentils. Simmer, serve over pasta.
- **N.V.:** High in plant-based protein and fiber.
- **Suggestions:** Great with a side salad or steamed vegetables.

Vegetable and Tofu Stir-Fry

- **P.T.:** 30 mins
- **Ingr.:** 1 block firm tofu (cubed), assorted vegetables (broccoli, bell pepper, carrot), 2 tbsp soy sauce, 1 tbsp sesame oil, 1 tsp ginger (grated), garlic (minced), rice or noodles.
- **Procedure:** Stir-fry tofu until golden. Add vegetables, soy sauce, sesame oil, ginger, and garlic. Serve with rice or noodles.
- **N.V.:** Rich in essential amino acids, vitamins, and minerals.
- **Suggestions:** Customize with your favorite vegetables.

Spinach and Ricotta Stuffed Shells

- **P.T.:** 1 hr
- **Ingr.:** Jumbo pasta shells, 1 cup vegan ricotta, 2 cups spinach (cooked, drained), 1/2 cup marinara sauce, nutritional yeast, salt, pepper, olive oil.
- **Procedure:** Cook pasta shells. Mix vegan ricotta, spinach, nutritional yeast, salt, and pepper. Stuff shells, place in baking dish, cover with sauce. Bake at 350°F.
- **N.V.:** High in calcium, iron, and fiber.
- **Suggestions:** Serve with a side of garlic bread and a fresh salad.

Vegan Snacks and Desserts

Cocoa and Almond Energy Bites

- **P.T.:** 20 mins (plus chilling)
- **Ingr.:** 1 cup rolled oats, 1/2 cup almond butter, 1/4 cup cocoa powder, 1/4 cup maple syrup, 1/4 cup chia seeds, a pinch of salt.
- **Procedure:** Mix all ingredients in a bowl. Form into small balls and refrigerate until firm.
- **N.V.:** High in fiber, healthy fats, and protein.
- **Suggestions:** A perfect snack for an energy boost during the day.

Vegan Avocado Chocolate Mousse

- **P.T.:** 15 mins
- **Ingr.:** 2 ripe avocados, 1/4 cup cocoa powder, 1/4 cup almond milk, 1/4 cup maple syrup, 1 tsp vanilla extract.
- **Procedure:** Blend avocados, cocoa powder, almond milk, maple syrup, and vanilla until smooth.
- **N.V.:** Rich in healthy fats and antioxidants.
- **Suggestions:** Serve chilled as a decadent yet healthy dessert.

Baked Apple Chips

- **P.T.:** 2 hrs 15 mins
- **Ingr.:** 2 apples, cinnamon, a sprinkle of sugar (optional).
- **Procedure:** Thinly slice apples, arrange on a baking sheet, sprinkle with cinnamon and sugar. Bake at 200°F until crisp.
- **N.V.:** Low in calories, high in fiber.
- **Suggestions:** A crunchy and sweet snack, perfect for midday cravings.

Spiced Roasted Chickpeas

- **P.T.:** 40 mins
- **Ingr.:** 1 can chickpeas (drained, rinsed), 1 tbsp olive oil, 1 tsp paprika, 1/2 tsp garlic powder, salt.
- **Procedure:** Toss chickpeas with olive oil, paprika, garlic powder, and salt. Roast at 400°F until crunchy.
- **N.V.:** Good source of protein and fiber.
- **Suggestions:** Great as a savory snack or salad topper.

Vegan Banana Nut Bread

- **P.T.:** 1 hr 10 mins
- **Ingr.:** 3 ripe bananas (mashed), 1/3 cup melted coconut oil, 1/2 cup maple syrup, 1/4 cup almond milk, 1 tsp vanilla extract, 1 tsp baking soda, a pinch of salt, 1 3/4 cups whole wheat flour, 1/2 cup walnuts (chopped).

- **Procedure:** Mix bananas, oil, syrup, milk, and vanilla. Add baking soda, salt, flour. Fold in walnuts. Bake in a lined loaf pan at 350°F.
- **N.V.:** Source of healthy fats, fiber, and essential nutrients.
- **Suggestions:** Enjoy as a breakfast treat or afternoon snack with tea.

Chapter 10: Gluten-Free Recipes

Gluten-Free Breakfasts

Buckwheat and Berry Breakfast Bowl

- **P.T.:** 20 mins
- **Ingr.:** 1/2 cup buckwheat groats, 1 cup almond milk, 1/2 cup mixed berries, 1 tbsp honey, 1 tsp cinnamon.
- **Procedure:** Cook buckwheat in almond milk until tender. Stir in honey and cinnamon. Top with berries.
- **N.V.:** High in fiber, gluten-free, and rich in antioxidants.
- **Suggestions:** Ideal for a nutritious and filling breakfast.

Quinoa Stuffed Bell Peppers

- **P.T.:** 45 mins
- **Ingr.:** 4 bell peppers, 1 cup quinoa (cooked), 1/2 cup black beans, 1/2 cup corn, 1/2 cup diced tomatoes, 1 tsp cumin, olive oil, salt, pepper.
- **Procedure:** Halve and deseed bell peppers. Mix quinoa, beans, corn, tomatoes, cumin, salt, and pepper. Stuff peppers, drizzle with olive oil, and bake.
- **N.V.:** Rich in protein and essential nutrients, gluten-free.
- **Suggestions:** Serve with a side salad or avocado slices.

Gluten-Free Chicken and Vegetable Stir-Fry

- **P.T.:** 30 mins
- **Ingr.:** 2 chicken breasts (sliced), 2 cups mixed vegetables (broccoli, carrots, bell peppers), 2 tbsp gluten-free soy sauce, 1 tbsp sesame oil, 1 tsp grated ginger, garlic (minced), olive oil.
- **Procedure:** Stir-fry chicken in olive oil, add vegetables, soy sauce, sesame oil, ginger, and garlic. Cook until veggies are tender.
- **N.V.:** High in protein, gluten-free, rich in vitamins.
- **Suggestions:** Serve over cooked rice or quinoa.

Almond Flour Banana Muffins

- **P.T.:** 35 mins
- **Ingr.:** 2 ripe bananas (mashed), 2 cups almond flour, 1/4 cup maple syrup, 2 eggs, 1 tsp baking powder, 1 tsp vanilla extract, a pinch of salt.
- **Procedure:** Combine all ingredients. Pour into muffin tins and bake at 350°F until golden.
- **N.V.:** Gluten-free, high in healthy fats and protein.
- **Suggestions:** Perfect for a snack or quick breakfast on the go.

Gluten-Free Seed and Nut Crackers

- **P.T.:** 1 hr 10 mins
- **Ingr.:** 1 cup mixed seeds (flax, sunflower, pumpkin), 1/2 cup nuts (almonds, walnuts), 1/2 cup water, 1 tbsp olive oil, salt, mixed herbs.
- **Procedure:** Blend seeds and nuts to a coarse mix. Add water, olive oil, salt, and herbs. Spread thinly on a baking sheet and bake until crispy.
- **N.V.:** Rich in omega-3 fatty acids, gluten-free.
- **Suggestions:** Pair with hummus or cheese for a satisfying snack.

Gluten-Free Lunches and Dinners

Grilled Portobello Mushroom Steaks

- **P.T.:** 30 mins
- **Ingr.:** 4 large portobello mushrooms, 2 tbsp olive oil, 1 tbsp balsamic vinegar, 2 cloves garlic (minced), thyme, salt, pepper.
- **Procedure:** Marinate mushrooms in olive oil, vinegar, garlic, thyme, salt, and pepper. Grill until tender.
- **N.V.:** High in fiber, vitamins, and antioxidants, gluten-free.
- **Suggestions:** Serve with a side of quinoa salad or roasted vegetables.

Zucchini Noodle Pad Thai

- **P.T.:** 20 mins
- **Ingr.:** 2 zucchinis (spiralized), 1 carrot (julienned), 1 bell pepper (thinly sliced), 1/4 cup peanuts, 2 tbsp tamari sauce (gluten-free), 1 tbsp lime juice, 1 tsp honey, 1 clove garlic (minced), cilantro.
- **Procedure:** Sauté vegetables. Mix tamari, lime juice, honey, and garlic for sauce. Combine with noodles, top with peanuts and cilantro.
- **N.V.:** Low-carb, rich in vitamins, gluten-free.
- **Suggestions:** Add tofu or shrimp for extra protein.

Cauliflower Crust Pizza

- **P.T.:** 45 mins
- **Ingr.:** 1 head cauliflower (riced), 1 egg, 1/2 cup mozzarella cheese (grated), 1 tsp Italian herbs, salt, pepper, tomato sauce, toppings of choice.
- **Procedure:** Mix cauliflower, egg, cheese, herbs, salt, and pepper. Form into crust, bake until golden. Add sauce and toppings, bake again.
- **N.V.:** Low in carbs, high in fiber, gluten-free.
- **Suggestions:** Customize with your favorite vegetables and protein.

Lentil Soup with Kale

- **P.T.:** 50 mins
- **Ingr.:** 1 cup lentils, 2 cups kale (chopped), 1 onion (chopped), 2 carrots (chopped), 2 cloves garlic (minced), vegetable broth, 1 tsp cumin, olive oil, salt, pepper.
- **Procedure:** Sauté onion, carrots, garlic. Add lentils, broth, cumin. Simmer until lentils are tender. Stir in kale until wilted.
- **N.V.:** High in plant protein, fiber, gluten-free.
- **Suggestions:** Perfect for a warming and nutritious meal.

Snacks and Treats Without Gluten

Coconut Flour Blueberry Muffins

- **P.T.:** 35 mins
- **Ingr.:** 3/4 cup coconut flour, 1/2 cup applesauce, 4 eggs, 1/4 cup honey, 1/2 tsp baking soda, 1 cup blueberries, 1 tsp vanilla extract, a pinch of salt.
- **Procedure:** Mix coconut flour, applesauce, eggs, honey, baking soda, vanilla, and salt. Fold in blueberries. Spoon into muffin tins and bake at 350°F.
- **N.V.:** High in fiber, protein, gluten-free.
- **Suggestions:** Enjoy as a breakfast treat or a healthy snack.

Almond Butter Fruit Dip

- **P.T.:** 10 mins
- **Ingr.:** 1/2 cup almond butter, 1/4 cup Greek yogurt, 1 tbsp maple syrup, 1/2 tsp cinnamon.
- **Procedure:** Mix all ingredients until smooth.
- **N.V.:** Rich in healthy fats, protein, gluten-free.
- **Suggestions:** Pair with apple slices, banana, or gluten-free crackers.

Roasted Pumpkin Seeds

- **P.T.:** 1 hr
- **Ingr.:** 1 cup pumpkin seeds (rinsed, dried), 1 tbsp olive oil, salt, paprika.
- **Procedure:** Toss seeds with oil, salt, and paprika. Roast at 300°F until crispy.
- **N.V.:** High in minerals, healthy fats, gluten-free.
- **Suggestions:** A crunchy snack, perfect for on-the-go.

Chocolate-Dipped Strawberries

- **P.T.:** 30 mins
- **Ingr.:** 1 cup strawberries, 1/2 cup dark chocolate chips (gluten-free), 1 tsp coconut oil.
- **Procedure:** Melt chocolate with coconut oil. Dip strawberries, place on parchment paper, refrigerate until set.
- **N.V.:** Rich in antioxidants, gluten-free.
- **Suggestions:** A delightful and elegant treat.

Gluten-Free Banana Bread

- **P.T.:** 1 hr 10 mins
- **Ingr.:** 3 ripe bananas (mashed), 2 cups gluten-free flour blend, 1/3 cup melted coconut oil, 1/2 cup honey, 2 eggs, 1/4 cup almond milk, 1 tsp baking powder, 1 tsp vanilla extract, a pinch of salt.
- **Procedure:** Combine bananas, oil, honey, eggs, milk, and vanilla. Add flour, baking powder, and salt. Pour into a loaf pan and bake at 325°F.
- **N.V.:** Source of healthy carbs, fiber, gluten-free.
- **Suggestions:** Serve with a cup of herbal tea as a comforting snack.

Chapter 11: Low-Sugar Recipes for Liver Health

Low-Sugar Breakfast Ideas

Avocado and Egg Toast on Sprouted Grain Bread

- **P.T.:** 15 mins
- **Ingr.:** 2 slices sprouted grain bread, 1 ripe avocado, 2 eggs, olive oil, salt, pepper, chili flakes (optional).
- **Procedure:** Toast bread. Fry eggs in olive oil. Mash avocado on toast, top with egg. Season with salt, pepper, and chili flakes.
- **N.V.:** High in healthy fats, protein, low in sugar.
- **Suggestions:** A filling and nutritious start to the day.

Greek Yogurt with Nuts and Berries

- **P.T.:** 10 mins
- **Ingr.:** 1 cup Greek yogurt (unsweetened), 1/4 cup mixed berries, 1/4 cup mixed nuts (almonds, walnuts), cinnamon.
- **Procedure:** Layer yogurt with berries and nuts. Sprinkle with cinnamon.
- **N.V.:** Rich in protein, healthy fats, low in sugar.
- **Suggestions:** Perfect for a quick and easy breakfast.

Spinach and Mushroom Omelette

- **P.T.:** 20 mins
- **Ingr.:** 3 eggs, 1 cup spinach (chopped), 1/2 cup mushrooms (sliced), 1 tbsp olive oil, salt, pepper, herbs (optional).
- **Procedure:** Sauté mushrooms, add spinach. Whisk eggs, pour over veggies. Cook until set, fold omelette.
- **N.V.:** High in protein, vitamins, low in sugar.
- **Suggestions:** Serve with a side of avocado or tomato slices.

Chia Seed and Almond Milk Pudding

- **P.T.:** Overnight (prep time 5 mins)
- **Ingr.:** 1/4 cup chia seeds, 1 cup almond milk (unsweetened), 1 tbsp almond butter, vanilla extract, stevia (optional), mixed berries.
- **Procedure:** Mix chia seeds, almond milk, almond butter, vanilla, and stevia. Refrigerate overnight. Top with berries.
- **N.V.:** High in omega-3 fatty acids, fiber, low in sugar.
- **Suggestions:** Customize with your favorite berries or nuts.

Satisfying Low-Sugar Lunches

Kale and Grilled Chicken Salad

- **P.T.:** 25 mins
- **Ingr.:** 2 cups kale (chopped), 1 chicken breast (grilled, sliced), 1/4 cup cherry tomatoes, 1/4 cup cucumber (sliced), 1 tbsp olive oil, 1 tbsp lemon juice, salt, pepper, 1/4 avocado (sliced).
- **Procedure:** Toss kale, tomatoes, cucumber in olive oil, lemon juice, salt, and pepper. Top with grilled chicken and avocado slices.
- **N.V.:** High in protein, essential nutrients, low in sugar.
- **Suggestions:** Ideal for a fulfilling and nutritious midday meal.

Broccoli and Almond Stir-Fry

- **P.T.:** 20 mins
- **Ingr.:** 2 cups broccoli florets, 1/4 cup almonds (slivered), 1 bell pepper (sliced), 1 tbsp sesame oil, 2 tbsp soy sauce (low sodium), 1 tsp ginger (grated), 1 clove garlic (minced).
- **Procedure:** Stir-fry broccoli, bell pepper, almonds in sesame oil. Add soy sauce, ginger, and garlic.
- **N.V.:** Rich in vitamins, minerals, low in sugar.
- **Suggestions:** Serve with brown rice or quinoa for a complete meal.

Lentil and Vegetable Soup

- **P.T.:** 40 mins
- **Ingr.:** 1 cup lentils, 1 carrot (chopped), 1 celery stalk (chopped), 1 onion (chopped), 2 cloves garlic (minced), 4 cups vegetable broth, 1 tsp thyme, olive oil, salt, pepper.

- **Procedure:** Sauté onion, carrot, celery, garlic in olive oil. Add lentils, broth, thyme. Simmer until lentils are tender.
- **N.V.:** High in plant-based protein, fiber, low in sugar.
- **Suggestions:** Enjoy with a slice of whole-grain bread.

Zucchini Noodle Caprese Salad

- **P.T.:** 15 mins
- **Ingr.:** 2 zucchinis (spiralized), 1/2 cup cherry tomatoes (halved), 1/4 cup mozzarella balls, 1/4 cup basil leaves, 1 tbsp balsamic vinegar, 2 tbsp olive oil, salt, pepper.

- **Procedure:** Combine zucchini noodles, tomatoes, mozzarella, basil. Dress with balsamic vinegar, olive oil, salt, and pepper.
- **N.V.:** Low in carbs, high in vitamins, low in sugar.
- **Suggestions:** A refreshing and light lunch, perfect for warm days.

Healthy, Low-Sugar Dinner Recipes

Herb-Roasted Turkey Breast

- **P.T.:** 1 hr 30 mins
- **Ingr.:** 1 boneless turkey breast (approx. 3 lbs), 1 tbsp olive oil, 2 cloves garlic (minced), 1 tsp rosemary, 1 tsp thyme, salt, pepper.
- **Procedure:** Rub turkey with olive oil, garlic, rosemary, thyme, salt, and pepper. Roast at 350°F until cooked through.
- **N.V.:** High in protein, low in sugar, rich in selenium.
- **Suggestions:** Serve with steamed green beans and a side salad.

Grilled Salmon with Asparagus

- **P.T.:** 25 mins
- **Ingr.:** 4 salmon fillets, 1 bunch asparagus, 1 lemon (sliced), 2 tbsp olive oil, salt, pepper, dill (optional).
- **Procedure:** Season salmon and asparagus with olive oil, salt, pepper. Grill alongside lemon slices. Garnish with dill.
- **N.V.:** Rich in omega-3 fatty acids, low in sugar, high in vitamins.
- **Suggestions:** Pair with a quinoa salad or roasted sweet potatoes.

Stuffed Bell Peppers with Cauliflower Rice

- **P.T.:** 45 mins
- **Ingr.:** 4 bell peppers (halved, seeded), 2 cups cauliflower rice, 1/2 cup diced tomatoes, 1 onion (chopped), 1 clove garlic (minced), 1 tsp cumin, olive oil, salt, pepper.
- **Procedure:** Sauté onion, garlic, add cauliflower rice, tomatoes, cumin, salt, and pepper. Stuff mixture into bell peppers. Bake at 375°F.
- **N.V.:** Low in carbs, high in fiber, low in sugar.
- **Suggestions:** Serve with a drizzle of avocado cream sauce.

Eggplant and Chickpea Curry

- **P.T.:** 40 mins
- **Ingr.:** 1 large eggplant (cubed), 1 can chickpeas (drained), 1 onion (chopped), 2 cloves garlic (minced), 1 can coconut milk, 1 tbsp curry powder, olive oil, salt, cilantro.
- **Procedure:** Sauté onion, garlic, add eggplant, chickpeas, curry powder, coconut milk, salt. Simmer until eggplant is tender. Garnish with cilantro.
- **N.V.:** High in plant-based protein, low in sugar.
- **Suggestions:** Serve over brown rice or with gluten-free naan bread.

Chapter 12: 10-Week Liver Detox Meal Plan

Week 1

Day	Breakfast	Snack	Lunch	Dinner
1	Green Detox Elixir	Kale Chips with Nutritional Yeast	Arugula and Beetroot Detox Salad	Stuffed Bell Peppers with Quinoa and Veggies
2	Mediterranean Morning Scramble	Carrot and Hummus Roll-Ups	Kale and Avocado Liver Support Salad	Herb-Crusted Salmon with Asparagus
3	Soy-Ginger Tofu Bowl	Spiced Chickpea Crunch	Quinoa and Edamame Liver Cleanse Bowl	Grilled Chicken with Mediterranean Quinoa
4	Almond Butter & Banana Chia Pudding	Apple Slices with Almond Butter	Detoxifying Spinach and Apple Salad	Curried Lentil and Sweet Potato Stew
5	Smoked Salmon and Avocado Omelette	Avocado and Tomato Rice Cakes	Citrus and Walnut Liver-Boosting Salad	Eggplant and Chickpea Ratatouille
6	Spiced Oat and Chia Porridge	Mango and Chia Seed Pudding	Miso Ginger Vegetable Soup	Lemon Garlic Tilapia with Zucchini Noodles
7	Tropical Buckwheat Bliss	Baked Cinnamon Apple Chips	Tuna and Avocado Lettuce Wraps	Quinoa Stuffed Acorn Squash

Week 2

Day	Breakfast	Snack	Lunch	Dinner
8	Berry Liver Cleanse Shake	Cinnamon Roasted Almonds	Spicy Tomato and Bean Soup	Spinach and Ricotta Stuffed Portobello Mushrooms
9	Beetroot Bliss Juice	Spicy Black Bean Dip	Tofu and Broccoli Stir-Fry	Roasted Cauliflower Steaks with Tahini Drizzle
10	Turmeric Sunrise Smoothie	Apple Slices with Almond Butter	Greek Yogurt and Berry Parfait	Lemon Herb Grilled Shrimp
11	Golden Millet Power Porridge	Roasted Red Pepper Hummus	Avocado Chickpea Salad Wrap	Soy-Glazed Salmon with Steamed Greens
12	Berry Walnut Muesli Mix	Mango and Chia Seed Pudding	Zesty Quinoa Tabbouleh	Farro and Mushroom Risotto
13	Avocado & Mint Refreshment	Kale Chips with Nutritional Yeast	Butternut Squash and Ginger Soup	Barley and Roasted Vegetable Medley
14	Quinoa & Black Bean Breakfast Wrap	Turmeric Spiced Walnuts	Chicken and Kale Detox Broth	Bulgur Wheat and Lentil Pilaf

Week 3

Day	Breakfast	Snack	Lunch	Dinner
15	Quinoa & Black Bean Breakfast Wrap	Roasted Red Pepper Hummus	Citrus and Walnut Liver-Boosting Salad	Roasted Vegetable Buddha Bowl
16	Smoked Salmon and Avocado Omelette	Kiwi and Pomegranate Salad	Tuna and Avocado Lettuce Wraps	Lemon Garlic Tilapia with Zucchini Noodles
17	Ancient Grains Liver Boost Bowl	Avocado and Tomato Rice Cakes	Spicy Black Bean Bowl	Turkey and Vegetable Skewers
18	Turmeric and Cinnamon Blend	Spiced Roasted Chickpeas	Miso Ginger Vegetable Soup	Whole Wheat Pasta with Kale and Pine Nuts
19	Berry Walnut Muesli Mix	Honey-Glazed Pecans with Sea Salt	Quinoa and Edamame Liver Cleanse Bowl	Bulgur Wheat and Lentil Pilaf
20	Ginger-Licorice Liver Elixir	Frozen Berry Yogurt Bites	Chicken and Kale Detox Broth	Zesty Lime Shrimp Zoodle Bowl
21	Spiced Oat and Chia Porridge	Baked Cinnamon Apple Chips	Greek Yogurt and Berry Parfait	Spinach and Ricotta Stuffed Shells

Week 4

Day	Breakfast	Snack	Lunch	Dinner
22	Turmeric and Cinnamon Blend	Honey-Glazed Pecans with Sea Salt	Detoxifying Spinach and Apple Salad	Grilled Chicken with Mediterranean Quinoa
23	Beetroot Bliss Juice	Creamy Avocado and Cilantro Dip	Butternut Squash and Ginger Soup	Spicy Shrimp and Veggie Stir-Fry
24	Almond Butter & Banana Chia Pudding	Frozen Berry Yogurt Bites	Lemon Herb Grilled Shrimp	Farro and Mushroom Risotto
25	Mediterranean Morning Scramble	Carrot and Hummus Roll-Ups	Avocado Chickpea Salad Wrap	Roasted Cauliflower Steaks with Tahini Drizzle
26	Soy-Ginger Tofu Bowl	Spiced Chickpea Crunch	Tofu and Broccoli Stir-Fry	Chickpea and Vegetable Stir-Fry
27	Spiced Oat and Chia Porridge	Kiwi and Pomegranate Salad	Greek Yogurt and Berry Parfait	Herb-Crusted Salmon with Asparagus
28	Berry Walnut Muesli Mix	Apple Slices with Almond Butter	Quinoa and Edamame Liver Cleanse Bowl	Lemon Garlic Tilapia with Zucchini Noodles

Week 5

Day	Breakfast	Snack	Lunch	Dinner
29	Avocado & Mint Refreshment	Spicy Black Bean Dip	Citrus and Walnut Liver-Boosting Salad	Grilled Chicken with Avocado Salad
30	Green Detox Elixir	Creamy Avocado and Cilantro Dip	Zesty Quinoa Tabbouleh	Whole Wheat Pasta with Kale and Pine Nuts
31	Smoked Salmon and Avocado Omelette	Mango and Chia Seed Pudding	Spiced Lentil Patty	Spicy Shrimp and Veggie Stir-Fry
32	Berry Liver Cleanse Shake	Baked Cinnamon Apple Chips	Greek Yogurt and Berry Parfait	Roasted Cauliflower Steaks with Tahini Drizzle
33	Golden Millet Power Porridge	Sesame and Flax Seed Crackers	Chicken and Kale Detox Broth	Soy-Glazed Salmon with Steamed Greens
34	Tropical Buckwheat Bliss	Sun-dried Tomato and Basil Pesto	Quinoa and Black Bean Salad	Lemon Garlic Tilapia with Zucchini Noodles
35	Almond Butter & Banana Chia Pudding	Cinnamon Roasted Almonds	Avocado Chickpea Salad Wrap	Stuffed Bell Peppers with Quinoa and Veggies

Week 6

Day	Breakfast	Snack	Lunch	Dinner
36	Avocado & Mint Refreshment	Roasted Pumpkin Seeds	Arugula and Beetroot Detox Salad	Zesty Lime Shrimp Zoodle Bowl
37	Berry Liver Cleanse Shake	Chia and Pumpkin Seed Trail Mix	Lemon Herb Grilled Shrimp	Stuffed Bell Peppers with Quinoa and Veggies
38	Turmeric Sunrise Smoothie	Avocado and Tomato Rice Cakes	Zesty Quinoa Tabbouleh	Quinoa Stuffed Acorn Squash
39	Ancient Grains Liver Boost Bowl	Honey-Glazed Pecans with Sea Salt	Tofu and Broccoli Stir-Fry	Roasted Vegetable Buddha Bowl
40	Soy-Ginger Tofu Bowl	Sun-dried Tomato and Basil Pesto	Greek Yogurt and Berry Parfait	Farro and Mushroom Risotto
41	Almond Butter & Banana Chia Pudding	Creamy Avocado and Cilantro Dip	Quinoa and Edamame Liver Cleanse Bowl	Bulgur Wheat and Lentil Pilaf
42	Spiced Oat and Chia Porridge	Apple Slices with Almond Butter	Spicy Black Bean Bowl	Lemon Garlic Tilapia with Zucchini Noodles

Week 7

Day	Breakfast	Snack	Lunch	Dinner
43	Green Detox Elixir	Spiced Chickpea Crunch	Kale and Avocado Liver Support Salad	Soy-Glazed Salmon with Steamed Greens
44	Mediterranean Morning Scramble	Kale Chips with Nutritional Yeast	Arugula and Beetroot Detox Salad	Whole Grain and Fiber-Rich Meals: Barley and Roasted Vegetable Medley
45	Quinoa & Black Bean Breakfast Wrap	Avocado and Tomato Rice Cakes	Detoxifying Spinach and Apple Salad	Chickpea and Vegetable Stir-Fry
46	Turmeric and Ginger Liver Tonic	Honey-Glazed Pecans with Sea Salt	Tuna and Avocado Lettuce Wraps	Spinach and Ricotta Stuffed Portobello Mushrooms
47	Berry Walnut Muesli Mix	Frozen Berry Yogurt Bites	Zesty Quinoa Tabbouleh	Grilled Chicken and Avocado Salad
48	Smoked Salmon and Avocado Omelette	Sesame and Flax Seed Crackers	Grilled Turmeric Chicken	Eggplant and Chickpea Ratatouille
49	Almond Butter & Banana Chia Pudding	Baked Cinnamon Apple Chips	Chicken and Kale Detox Broth	Farro and Mushroom Risotto

Week 8

Day	Breakfast	Snack	Lunch	Dinner
50	Beetroot Bliss Juice	Carrot and Hummus Roll-Ups	Chicken and Kale Detox Broth	Eggplant Chickpea Tagine
51	Avocado & Mint Refreshment	Kiwi and Pomegranate Salad	Citrus and Walnut Liver-Boosting Salad	Quinoa Stuffed Acorn Squash
52	Tropical Buckwheat Bliss	Spiced Chickpea Crunch	Spicy Black Bean Bowl	Grilled Chicken with Mediterranean Quinoa
53	Golden Millet Power Porridge	Baked Cinnamon Apple Chips	Quinoa and Edamame Liver Cleanse Bowl	Zesty Lime Shrimp Zoodle Bowl
54	Berry Liver Cleanse Shake	Chia and Pumpkin Seed Trail Mix	Tofu and Broccoli Stir-Fry	Roasted Cauliflower Steaks with Tahini Drizzle
55	Mediterranean Morning Scramble	Apple Slices with Almond Butter	Miso Ginger Vegetable Soup	Whole Wheat Pasta with Kale and Pine Nuts
56	Almond Butter & Banana Chia Pudding	Turmeric Spiced Walnuts	Avocado Chickpea Salad Wrap	Farro and Mushroom Risotto

Week 9

Day	Breakfast	Snack	Lunch	Dinner
57	Green Tea and Hibiscus Blend	Spicy Black Bean Dip	Detoxifying Spinach and Apple Salad	Curried Lentil and Sweet Potato Stew
58	Berry Liver Cleanse Shake	Pineapple and Cottage Cheese Bowl	Tofu and Broccoli Stir-Fry	Grilled Portobello Mushroom Steaks
59	Soy-Ginger Tofu Bowl	Creamy Avocado and Cilantro Dip	Zesty Quinoa Tabbouleh	Roasted Cauliflower Steaks with Tahini Drizzle
60	Spiced Oat and Chia Porridge	Sesame and Flax Seed Crackers	Spiced Lentil Patty	Lemon Garlic Tilapia with Zucchini Noodles
61	Quinoa & Black Bean Breakfast Wrap	Baked Cinnamon Apple Chips	Greek Yogurt and Berry Parfait	Zesty Lime Shrimp Zoodle Bowl
62	Tropical Buckwheat Bliss	Kale Chips with Nutritional Yeast	Miso Ginger Vegetable Soup	Bulgur Wheat and Lentil Pilaf
63	Almond Butter & Banana Chia Pudding	Honey-Glazed Pecans with Sea Salt	Avocado Chickpea Salad Wrap	Chickpea and Vegetable Stir-Fry

Week 10

Day	Breakfast	Snack	Lunch	Dinner
64	Avocado & Mint Refreshment	Frozen Berry Yogurt Bites	Butternut Squash and Ginger Soup	Soy-Glazed Salmon with Steamed Greens
65	Golden Millet Power Porridge	Mango and Chia Seed Pudding	Chicken and Kale Detox Broth	Chickpea and Vegetable Stir-Fry
66	Spiced Oat and Chia Porridge	Spiced Chickpea Crunch	Spicy Tomato and Bean Soup	Lemon Garlic Tilapia with Zucchini Noodles
67	Berry Liver Cleanse Shake	Cinnamon Roasted Almonds	Quinoa and Edamame Liver Cleanse Bowl	Zesty Lime Shrimp Zoodle Bowl
68	Turmeric Sunrise Smoothie	Apple Slices with Almond Butter	Arugula and Beetroot Detox Salad	Grilled Chicken with Mediterranean Quinoa
69	Almond Butter & Banana Chia Pudding	Kale Chips with Nutritional Yeast	Tuna and Avocado Lettuce Wraps	Stuffed Bell Peppers with Quinoa and Veggies
70	Smoked Salmon and Avocado Omelette	Carrot and Hummus Roll-Ups	Zesty Quinoa Tabbouleh	Bulgur Wheat and Lentil Pilaf

Chapter 13: Continuing Your Liver Health Journey

Adapting Recipes for Long-Term Liver Health

As you journey through the continuous path of maintaining and enhancing liver health, the adaptation of recipes to suit a long-term liver-friendly diet becomes an art and science of its own. This enduring commitment to your liver's wellbeing involves not just an understanding of what is beneficial or detrimental to liver health, but also the creative integration of these insights into daily meals.

To start, consider the fundamental components of your meals. Whole, unprocessed foods should form the cornerstone of your diet. But beyond that, think about how you can enhance these ingredients. Incorporating herbs and spices not only elevates taste but also offers significant health benefits. Turmeric, for instance, is renowned for its anti-inflammatory properties, while cinnamon can help regulate blood sugar levels. These small yet impactful additions make a substantial difference in the long-term nurturing of your liver.

Furthermore, the method of preparation plays a crucial role. Grilling, baking, or steaming are preferable to frying or other high-fat cooking methods. These techniques preserve the integrity of the nutrients while minimizing the introduction of harmful fats and toxins. Additionally, being mindful of portion sizes ensures that you're not overloading your liver with more than it can comfortably handle.

Moreover, as you adapt recipes, keep an eye on sodium, sugar, and unhealthy fat content. These are often the hidden culprits in many dishes. Opting for natural sweeteners, using herbs for flavoring instead of salt, and choosing unsaturated fats over saturated or trans fats are all strategies that can substantially benefit liver health.

Tips for Eating Out and Social Events

Navigating the social world while maintaining a commitment to your liver health can be challenging, yet it is entirely possible with the right strategies and mindset. When dining out or attending social events, the key is to make informed choices that align with your liver health journey, ensuring you can enjoy these experiences without compromising your well-being.

When planning to dine out, research is your ally. Most restaurants now offer their menus online, allowing you to peruse options ahead of time. Look for dishes that are rich in vegetables, lean proteins, and whole grains, and don't be afraid to ask for modifications. Most establishments are more than willing to accommodate requests such as grilling instead of frying or substituting a side of vegetables for fries. This proactive approach ensures that when you sit down to order, you're well-informed and can make choices that are delicious and liver-friendly.

Moreover, consider portion control as an effective tool. Restaurant servings are often more generous than what you might serve at home. You can ask for a half portion or share a dish with a friend. Alternatively, consider packing half of your meal to go right from the start, ensuring you don't overindulge. This strategy allows you to enjoy the flavors and experience of dining out without overloading your liver.

Be beverage savvy. Alcoholic drinks can be particularly taxing on your liver, and sugary beverages offer no nutritional benefit. Opt for water, herbal tea, or if you choose to drink alcohol, select one glass of red wine known for its antioxidants. Being mindful of your beverage choice is a simple yet effective way to support liver health while enjoying social occasions.

When attending events or parties, don't go hungry. Eating a healthy snack before heading out can prevent overindulgence. Once there, scan the buffet or menu for the healthiest options, and fill your plate with these first. Vegetables, fruits, nuts, and seeds are often available and can be a great starting point. Engage in conversations away from the buffet or table, reducing the temptation to eat mindlessly.

Monitoring Your Liver Health Progress

As you navigate the path to sustained liver health, vigilance in tracking your progress becomes as crucial as the lifestyle changes you've adopted. Monitoring your liver's condition is a nuanced endeavor that goes beyond periodic assessments—it's an integral part of a holistic approach to health, empowering you with the knowledge to tailor your journey effectively.

Beginning with the clinical aspect, regular medical evaluations stand as the bedrock of effective monitoring. Engaging with healthcare professionals for routine liver function tests illuminates the impact of your dietary and lifestyle modifications. These tests, examining elements like enzyme levels and bilirubin, offer quantifiable insights into the liver's state. When these numbers shift, they whisper stories of improvement or caution, guiding the tweaks in your regimen.

In the era of digital health, leveraging technological advancements can significantly enhance your monitoring strategy. Apps designed to track nutritional intake, physical activity, and even hydration levels act as daily companions on your health journey. They transform abstract goals into tangible data, allowing you to see patterns and progress, or lack thereof, in real time. This constant stream of information serves as both a motivator and a guide, helping you to stay committed and make informed decisions.

Listening to your body is an art that complements the science of health monitoring. Subtle changes in well-being, energy levels, or even skin condition can signal shifts in liver health. Cultivating an awareness of these bodily cues encourages a more responsive and personalized approach to health. It's about becoming fluent in the language your body speaks, understanding that symptoms or improvements are its way of communicating needs and successes.

Periodic imaging tests, such as ultrasounds or CT scans, provide a visual dimension to monitoring, revealing the liver's structure and any physical changes. These snapshots capture what numbers and symptoms can't, offering a comprehensive view of your liver's health. They can detect alterations in tissue, signs of inflammation, or scarring, providing critical information that shapes the course of treatment or maintenance.

Yet, the journey doesn't stop at medical interventions and technological aids. Reflecting on your emotional and psychological well-being is equally vital. Stress, motivation levels, and mental health significantly impact physiological health, including liver function. Regularly checking in with yourself, perhaps through journaling or mindfulness practices, ensures that you're not just surviving but thriving as you make these life-long changes.

Patience is the unsung hero of any health journey, especially when it comes to the liver, an organ that quietly bears much of the body's burdens. Improvements might unfold slowly, and setbacks may occur. Celebrating the incremental victories and understanding the setbacks as learning opportunities rather than defeats fortify your resolve and commitment.

Beyond Diet: Holistic Approaches to Liver Health

Embracing a broader perspective, one that includes a variety of lifestyle strategies, is crucial for nurturing and sustaining the liver's well-being. This comprehensive approach not only addresses physical health but also encompasses emotional and spiritual aspects, recognizing the interconnectedness of our entire being.

Physical activity emerges as a significant ally in the quest for liver health. Regular exercise helps to decrease liver fat, combat obesity, and improve insulin sensitivity, all of which are beneficial for the liver. Whether it's a brisk walk, a cycle through the park, or a yoga session, the key is consistency and enjoyment, ensuring that this becomes an integral and sustainable part of your lifestyle.

Transitioning into the realm of stress management, the importance of this aspect cannot be overstated. Chronic stress has been shown to have adverse effects on the liver, exacerbating conditions like fatty liver disease and hindering overall liver function. Adopting stress-reduction techniques such as meditation, deep breathing exercises, or engaging in hobbies can significantly mitigate stress, thereby supporting liver health.

Moreover, adequate and quality sleep is a cornerstone of liver health. During sleep, the body's repair processes are activated, including those of the liver. Ensuring a regular sleep schedule, creating a restful environment, and adopting pre-sleep relaxation techniques can enhance the quality of sleep, contributing to the liver's ability to rejuvenate and detoxify effectively.

Considering the impact of environmental toxins is crucial. Exposure to certain chemicals and pollutants can overburden the liver, impeding its ability to function efficiently. Being mindful of the products you use, from household cleaners to personal care items, and opting for natural, non-toxic alternatives can reduce the liver's toxic load.

Made in United States
Troutdale, OR
01/24/2025

28276294R00064